Mushrooms and toadstools belong to the fungal kingdom. There are about 4,000 species of larger fungi in Britain. Of the larger umbrella-shaped fungi with a cap and stem, mushroom is a popular term for those that are edible; toadstool for those that are poisonous.

A fungus is not a plant. Most plants make food using the sun's energy. Animals and fungi need a food source, usually plant or animal, living or dead. Animals digest food internally. In fungi enzymes dissolve the food externally from where it is absorbed.

Plants and animals are made up of many tiny cells, but mushrooms and toadstools are composed of very thin tubes known as hyphae. As a hypha grows it branches and produces a web of threads known as a mycelium. This is the equivalent of stems, roots and leaves in a plant. On a flat surface it often grows as an expanding disc and this shape is clearly seen in simple fungi such as moulds on food.

Unlike moulds, mushrooms and toadstools reproduce by forming spores in large fruitbodies. These are the structures that are described in this book and frequently the rest of the fungus is hidden from view. A fruitbody may only exist for a few days before rotting away but the mycelium which produces it may live for years and some individuals are known to be hundreds of years old.

Where do fungi grow?

Many species described in this book are found among short, mown or grazed grass. Such fungi feed on dead plant or animal material present in the soil. Undisturbed pasture that has not been ploughed or had chemical fertilisers applied is usually much richer in fungi than reseeded grass that has been limed and fertilised.

Lawns and playing fields are often carefully prepared, with the soil being riddled to remove stones, and as such provide perfect sites for the growth of 'fairy rings' – the appearance of a ring of fruitbodies. In the past these were explained away by references to toads or fairies but in fact they result from fruitbodies being produced at the growing edge of the buried mycelium which under uniform soil conditions grows as a circular disc. As the mycelium grows so the size of the circle increases.

Grazed grassland attracts species of fungi that feed on dung. Horse and cow dung is especially rich in fungi, though many have small fruitbodies. Larger species include Dung Roundhead (p.119) and Egghead Mottlegill (p.148).

Woodlands are home to a wide range of fungi. In addition to species growing in woodland soil there are those that rot tree leaves (including conifer needles), those that rot fallen wood and old stumps, and those that feed on living trees. Of the latter, some enter as germinating spores through a wound and the mycelium spreads before producing bracket-like fruitbodies from the trunk. Others invade via the tree roots and form a web or mycorrhiza (fungus root). Such fungi draw food from tree roots but produce terrestrial fruitbodies, though some (e.g. truffles) produce them underground.

Mushrooms

Patrick Harding
Photographs by Alan Outen

HarperCollins*Publishers*

77–85 Fulham Palace Road, Hammersmith, London W6 8JB

First published 1996

Second edition published 2003. Reprinted with amendments 2008

This edition published 2013

12

The copyright in the photographs belongs to Alan Outen except for the following: Patrick Harding 26, 63, 66, 70, 72, 82, 99, 100, 115, 124, 148, 151, 156, 157, 159, 168, 169, 181, 185, 191, 200, 206, 220, 233, 235, 238, 243; Guillaume Eyssartier 17; Jacques Vast 19, 49, 71, 77, 90, 96, 127, 209, 215, 227, 241; G. Redeuilh 40, 62, 65, 98, 108, 111, 141, 195; S. Clelland 41, 167; G. Dickson 50; Bob Gibbons 53, 130, 171, 180, 193, 197, 219; John Roberts 80, 94, 102, 190, 192, 205, 217, 224, 226; N. Niserens 221, 225; Gérard Martin 89, 245; A. Wason 117; K. Rowland 133; René Chalange 155; Pascal Hériveau 178, 223, 242; Robert Le Coz 101, 199.

Artwork is by John Wilkinson

ISBN 978-0-00-718307-4

Printed in China by South China Printing Co. Ltd

Many fungi are restricted to one or a small number of tree species. Yellow Stagshorn (p.209) grows on pine stumps and also on spruce. Hen of the Woods (p.197) typically grows at the base of oak trees. Mycorrhizal species are especially host specific and their names often relate to this, e.g. Brown Birch Bolete (p.160) and Beechwood Sickener (p.86). Some tree species have a large number of associated species of fungi and among those with the most are oak, beech, birch and Scots pine.

Other habitats include gardens and parks. More specific places include cellars, wood stacks, old bonfire sites and manure heaps. Some fungi, e.g. Ergot (p.242), grow from grass flowers, while others emerge from the bodies of animals they have killed.

Edible and Poisonous Fungi

Many edible fungi have 'lookalikes' that may be poisonous. This is even true for the Field Mushroom, the most commonly consumed wild fungus in Britain. Beginners must on no account gather wild fungi to eat unless they have been correctly identified by an expert. The publishers and the author cannot accept responsibility for any identification of a mushroom or plant made by the users of this book. Although many species are edible for many people, some species cause allergic reactions or illness for certain individuals. These are totally unpredictable, therefore the publishers and the author cannot take responsibility for any effects resulting from eating any wild foods. It is recommended that you consult your GP immediately if you experience such a reaction.

Collecting and identifying fungi

Some fungi cannot be identified without a microscope but most of the species in this book can be named using macro characters. Collect the whole fungus (using a knife if necessary) and place in a basket. Fragile species are best put in small boxes. Make notes about habitat, e.g. 'growing on a stump' or 'under birch' and remember that a slimy texture or faint smell may dry or fade.

In this book descriptions concentrate on characters of the fruitbody, including colour (which is very variable), shape (which often changes as the fruitbody matures – note, a raised central region is known as an umbo), smell and texture. Most species are umbrella- or mushroom-shaped and have gills on the cap underside, like shop mushrooms.

Gill characters are important, especially the way they are attached to the stem. This is best seen by slicing the cap in half.

Gill Characteristics

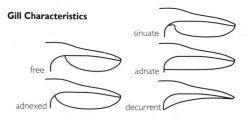

sinuate

free

adnate

adnexed

decurrent

A spore print (the colour of a mass of spores) is very important for accurate identification. Remove stem and put the cap gills (or tubes) down on a piece of glass. Cover to keep moist and leave for at least 4 hours, after which there should be a white or coloured deposit.

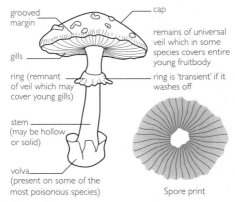

grooved margin

cap

remains of universal veil which in some species covers entire young fruitbody

gills

ring (remnant of veil which may cover young gills)

ring is 'transient' if it washes off

stem (may be hollow or solid)

volva (present on some of the most poisonous species)

Spore print

Species entries

The information provided is arranged as follows:

- A symbol – see pp.9–12 for explanation
- The spore colour (within the circle) of the species.
- The family or group to which the species belongs.
- The English name of the species. These follow *List of Recommended English Names for Fungi* (2003).

● The Latin name of the species. As with flowering plants this binomial is printed in italics. The first word indicates the genus to which the fungus belongs. The second word is the species name. As with other organisms Latin names can change, especially as modern research improves our knowledge of the relationship between species. Names follow *Checklist of the British & Irish Basidiomycota* (2005) by Legon & Henrici.

● The main paragraph gives background details and lists the most important features to aid identification. Features are described in order: cap, gills (where present) and stem. Features that cannot be shown in the photograph such as texture and smell are also listed here.

SIZE This gives the normal range. The measures are (usually) for cap diameter, stem height and stem width.

HABITAT An important section, as some fungi are only found in very restricted habitats.

SEASON This gives the usual fruiting season, but remember that unusual weather conditions may cause fruitbodies to appear at odd times.

POISONOUS Edible, Inedible, Poisonous (red = Very Poisonous) An indication of possible culinary use is given but beginners should avoid gathering and eating wild fungi without an expert having identified them first.

SIMILAR SPECIES This section includes both closely related species (usually in the same genus) and species that look similar and may confuse a beginner.

At each number there is a range of alternative descriptions – choose the one that most closely fits your specimen. This will direct you to the next key stage or to a page number.

1 FRUITBODY SHAPE

   a Grows on wood like a crust, shelf or bracket
      with no stem or a laterally attached stem   **see 2**
   b Finger, club, antler or coral shape   **see 3**
   c Spherical, star or nest shape   **see 4**
   d Ear, saddle, brain or cauliflower shape   **see 5**
   e Disc, saucer or cup shape   **see 6**
   f Umbrella shape with cap and central stem   **see 7**

2 CRUST, SHELF OR BRACKET-LIKE

   a Gills on the underside   165, 170–173
   b Smooth underside;   181–183
      bracket < 7cm across, < 1cm thick
   c Tiny pores or folds underneath;   184–187
      bracket < 7cm across, < 1cm thick
   d Round, angular or slit-like pores;   188–197, 199, 201, 202
      bracket >7cm across, >1cm thick

3 FINGER, CLUB, ANTLER OR CORAL SHAPE

   a Jelly-like texture   207–209
   b Brittle or hard texture   **see c or d**
   c Unbranched, finger or club shape
      1 Brittle texture   174, 240–241
      2 Hard texture   242, 245, 246

7 UMBRELLA SHAPE WITH CENTRALLY ATTACHED STEM
   CAP WITH:

	a	Teeth on underside	178–179
	b	Pores on underside	150–163, 198, 200
	c	Smooth or wrinkled underside	167–169
	d	Gills on underside	**see 8**

8 MUSHROOMS AND TOADSTOOLS WITH GILLS
   SPORE COLOUR:

a	*Pink* ●	
	1 Gills free, on rotting wood	101–102
	2 Gills not free	27–28, 103–109
b	*Brown* ● ●	
	1 In grass, small and fragile	110–111, 131
	2 In grass, medium sized, with ring	112
	3 Woodland species	121–130
c	*Brown* ● ● ●	
	1 Gills free	132–136
	2 Gills not free	113–120, 164
d	*Black* ●	
	1 Inky fluid from old gills	137–142
	2 No inky fluid, plain gills	143–145
	3 No inky fluid, mottled gills	146–149
e	*White* (or very pale colour) ○	**see 9**

9 MUSHROOMS AND TOADSTOOLS WITH WHITE SPORES
(including white, cream and pale yellow spores)

a	Gills free	
	1 Volva at stem base	13–20
	2 No volva, ring on stem	21–23
	Gills not free	**see b**
b	Gills thick, waxy, mostly in grass	66–73
	Gills not thick and waxy	**see c**
c	Fruitbody easily crumbled, woodland spp	**see d**
	Fruitbody not easily crumbled	**see e**
d	No milky fluid from damaged gills	74–88
	Damaged gills exude milky fluid	89–100
e	Ring present on stem	24, 53, 55–56
	Ring absent	**see f**
f	Bell-shaped cap, slender stem	42–49
	Convex, flat or funnel-shaped cap	**see g**
g	Gills decurrent	25–26, 29–33, 50–51, 166
	Gills sinuate	57–62, 64–65
	Gills adnate or adnexed	**see h**
h	Cap < 1.5cm, on twigs, leaves or needles	40–41
	Cap > 1.5cm across	**see i**
i	Stem pliable, not easily broken	34–39, 52, 54
	Stems fusing, clustered fruitbodies	63

A striking, commonly found fungus often depicted
in fairy-tale illustrations and on greeting cards.
It was traditionally used as a fly killer. The
entire young fruitbody is enclosed in a white veil
that leaves fragments (which may wash off) on the
shiny red, marginally grooved cap. The gills are white and
free, the ring hanging and grooved. The stem base is
swollen with rings of scales (remains of volva, see p.7).

SIZE Cap 10–20 cm, stem 15–20 cm x 15–20 mm.
HABITAT Mostly with birch; also with pine and spruce.
SEASON Late summer to early winter.
POISONOUS Rarely fatal. Hallucinogenic properties.
SIMILAR SPECIES The edible Caesar's Mushroom (*A. caesarea*)
has an orange-red, mostly unspotted cap, yellow stem and
gills and a sack-like volva. Not found in Britain.

Uncommon but often confused with Grey Spotted Amanita (p.15), its ochre-brown cap has a grooved margin and regular pattern of white, warty veil fragments (these may wash off). The gills are white and free, the ring ungrooved and pendulous. The white stem has several scaly rings above the eggcup-like swollen base.

SIZE Cap 5–10 cm, stem 6–10 cm x 10–20 mm.
HABITAT Usually with beech or oak woodland.
SEASON Summer to autumn.
POISONOUS Can be fatal if consumed.
SIMILAR SPECIES Grey Spotted Amanita (p.15) differs in its grey cap spots, less obvious volva and grooves on the upper surface of the ring. Blusher (p.16) also has ring grooves and a less obvious volva but flesh-coloured cap spots.

The flat grey-brown cap is covered with irregular pale grey patches from the remains of the veil that enclosed the young fruitbody. The gills are free and white. The stem is white with a transient ring that is grooved on the upper surface. The swollen base has bands of scales but no enclosing sack. Smell of radish.

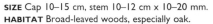

SIZE Cap 10–15 cm, stem 10–12 cm x 10–20 mm.
HABITAT Broad-leaved woods, especially oak.
SEASON Summer to early autumn.
POISONOUS Easily confused with poisonous species and so not recommended.
SIMILAR SPECIES Panthercap (p.14) differs in its white cap patches, ungrooved ring and rimmed top to the swollen stem base.

Amanita rubescens

The rounded cap is initially covered with the off-white veil that leaves remnants on the flatter, older cap. The remnants are grey, flesh-coloured or pale yellow and are later widely spaced, if present at all. The underlying cap colour ranges from cream to dark brown. The white gills and flesh bruise pinky-red. The broad white stem has a bulbous base and is flecked rosy-brown below the white, grooved ring.

SIZE Cap 5–15 cm, stem 7–15 cm x 10–25 mm.
HABITAT Broad-leaved woods, usually with birth.
SEASON Early summer to autumn.
EDIBLE Must be well cooked. Causes anaemia if eaten raw.
SIMILAR SPECIES Confused with Panthercap, Grey Spotted Amanita and Deathcap (pp.14, 15 & 17), none of which turn pinky-red on bruising or cutting.

One of the most poisonous of all fungi; it has caused many fatalities. After bursting through the white veil the shiny, olive-yellow to greeny-bronze flattened cap is usually devoid of veil fragments. The gills are white and crowded, the white ring grooved and pendulous. The white stem has faint, wavy cap-coloured zones. The base is encased in a white, sack-like volva. It has an unpleasant smell when old.

SIZE Cap 5–12 cm, stem 10–12 cm x 10–20 mm.
HABITAT Broad-leaved woods, especially with oak or beech.
SEASON Midsummer to late autumn.
POISONOUS Causes liver and kidney failure.
SIMILAR SPECIES Confused with False Deathcap (p.18), which is paler, has no sack-like volva and smells strongly of radish.

False Deathcap

AMANITACEAE FAMILY

Amanita citrina

The cap is pale lemon with irregular ochre-yellow veil fragments. Also common as a white form (var. *alba*). The gills are white and free. The stem is paler than the cap, with a white ring grooved on the upper surface, as is the stem apex. There is a trough-like volva at the bulbous stem base. It smells of raw potato or radish.

SIZE Cap 4–9 cm, stem 5–7 cm x 10–15 mm.
HABITAT Mostly with birch, beech and oak.
SEASON Midsummer to autumn.
EDIBLE Not recommended as too easily confused with poisonous species (see opposite).
SIMILAR SPECIES Deathcap (p.17) is darker; Destroying Angel (p.19) is whiter; both lack the sharp smell.

The cap is initially hidden in the white veil, which is cast off to reveal a smooth, slightly sticky, bell-shaped cap with crowded, white, free gills. The slender white, often curved stem bears loose scales and a large transient ring just below the cap. The base is enclosed in a white sack-like volva. It has a sickly sweet smell.

SIZE Cap 5–10 cm, stem 10–15 cm x 10–15 mm.
HABITAT In open broad-leaved woodland.
SEASON Late summer to autumn.
POISONOUS Symptoms like those from Deathcap.
SIMILAR SPECIES The pale form of False Deathcap (p.18) lacks the sack-like volva. Mushrooms (pp.132–136) lack a volva and have pink gills with dark brown spores.

Tawny Grisette

AMANITACEAE
FAMILY

Amanita fulva

Unlike other common Amanitas, this and the similar, less common, Grisette have no ring. Expanding through a white veil, the shiny cap (sticky when moist) is orange-brown with a darker, raised centre and grooved margin. It has white, free gills. The smooth white stem is flushed with the cap colour and narrows towards the apex. The white sack-like volva encloses the stem base.

SIZE Cap 4–8 cm, stem 10–15 cm x 10–15 mm.
HABITAT Broad-leaved woods, especially with birch.
SEASON Midsummer to autumn.
EDIBLE Must be well cooked. Not recommended.
SIMILAR SPECIES Grisette (*A. vaginata*) is slightly larger and has a grey to grey-brown cap. Usually with beech or oak.

When young, it is shaped like an egg on a stick but the mature cap is flat, apart from a raised, dark-brown central region that is surrounded by rings of flat brown scales on a cream background. It has dry, creamy-white gills. The long, hollow stem tapers from a swollen base and bears faint snake-like markings below the movable double ring.

SIZE Cap 10–25 cm, stem 15–35 cm x 15–25 mm.
HABITAT Meadows, parks, verges, open woodland.
SEASON Midsummer to late autumn.
EDIBLE Excellent nutty taste. Discard stem and fry the cap whole, coated in breadcrumbs.
SIMILAR SPECIES Often confused with Shaggy Parasol (p.22). Slender Parasol (*M. mastoidea*) is half the size with tiny pale-brown cap scales and a creamy stem.

Chlorophyllum (Macrolepiota) rhacodes

Frequently confused with Parasol, it is smaller but stockier and has a more convex, fleshier cap covered with pale-beige scales that bend away from the cap. The stem lacks snake-like markings. The cap and stem flesh, together with the cream-coloured gills, turn orange-red when cut. It has a strong, slightly sweet smell.

SIZE Cap 12–18 cm, stem 8–12 cm x 15–20 mm.
HABITAT Most frequent under conifers.

SEASON Midsummer to late autumn.
EDIBLE A minority suffer from digestive upset and skin rash.
SIMILAR SPECIES *C. brunneum* has a stouter stem and cap covered with chestnut-coloured scales. Associated with rich garden soil and compost heaps.

The small, bell-shaped cap matures flat but with a raised red-brown centre surrounded by rings of small, similar-coloured scales on a pinky-white ground. The very crowded, free white gills age browner. The slender, silky-white stem bears a small transient ring. Unpleasant smell of rubber or tar.

SIZE Cap 2–5 cm, stem 3–6 cm x 3–4 mm.
HABITAT In lawns and pastures and among woodland litter.
SEASON Late summer to autumn.
POISONOUS Many closely related species are very poisonous, so do not eat small 'Parasols'.
SIMILAR SPECIES Less common species include those with white, olive or dark-brown cap-scales and those with a fruity smell. Some are very poisonous.

Cystoderma amianthinum

Similar to the small Lepiotas, e.g. Stinking Dapperling (p.23), but with gills attached to the stem. The thin-fleshed, ochre-yellow cap has a granular surface and a shaggy edge. It has adnate, creamy-white gills. The slender, cap-coloured stem is unusual in that the lower region (below the shaggy, often incomplete ring) is covered with tiny scales. It has an earthy smell.

SIZE Cap 2–5 cm, stem 4–7 cm x 3–4 mm.

HABITAT Among moss and grass in acid pastures and heaths. Also in broad-leaved and coniferous woods on acid soil.

SEASON Late summer to autumn.

INEDIBLE Not worthwhile.

SIMILAR SPECIES *C. carcharias* is pinky-grey and is commonest under pine or spruce.

A common woodland species often occurring in large troops. The cap is flat or slightly depressed, pinky-brown, drying paler. It has a granular central region and a striate edge when moist. The gills are flesh-coloured, adnate to slightly decurrent, thick and widely spaced. The stem is thin, fibrous and often flattened.

SIZE Cap 1–4 cm, stem 3–10 cm x 2–5 mm.
HABITAT Among tree leaf litter and on heaths.
SEASON Late summer to autumn.
EDIBLE Lacking in flavour. Discard the tough stems.
SIMILAR SPECIES Closely related species include the larger *L. proxima* growing on peaty soil and the paler *L. bicolor* with a lilac stem base. Toughshanks (pp.35 to 38) have crowded gills.

Often found in large troops. When young and moist, the cap, stem and gills are deep violet. The cap and stem mature pale buff, the widely spaced gills to white. The cap edge is often wavy or split, the centre is slightly rough and often darker. The tough stem is frequently bent or twisted.

SIZE Cap 1–4 cm, stem 4–8 cm x 3–6 mm.
HABITAT On soil under broad-leaved trees, mostly among beech litter.
SEASON Autumn or late summer to early winter.
EDIBLE Retains its colour when cooked but lacks flavour. Deceiver (p.25) is similar but is red-brown.
SIMILAR SPECIES Lilac Bonnet (p.47) is rosy-lilac with grey-tinged gills and smells of radish. The lilac form of White Fibrecap (p.126) has brown gills.

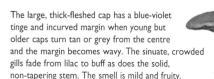

The large, thick-fleshed cap has a blue-violet tinge and incurved margin when young but older caps turn tan or grey from the centre and the margin becomes wavy. The sinuate, crowded gills fade from lilac to buff as does the solid, non-tapering stem. The smell is mild and fruity.

SIZE Cap 5–15 cm, stem 5–10 cm x 15–25 mm.
HABITAT In leaf litter of woods, hedgerows and gardens. Also in grasslands away from trees.
SEASON Autumn to late winter.
EDIBLE Must be well cooked. Watery when old.
SIMILAR SPECIES Field Blewit (p.28) lacks the lilac cap and gills. *L. sordida* has a darker cap colour and smells of bitter almonds. Violet species of *Cortinarius* (e.g. *C. purpurascens* p.122) have rusty-brown spores.

The large cap is initially convex with an inrolled edge, later flat or concave. It is pale, grey-brown, thick and fleshy. The grey-pink gills are sinuate and crowded. The short, thick stem is streaked bright violet, especially near its base, which is often swollen.

SIZE Cap 5–12 cm, stem 4–10 cm x 15–25 mm.
HABITAT Grassland and woodland edges, often in rings.
SEASON Autumn to early winter.
EDIBLE Stem and cap have firm flesh and a subtle taste. Dries well.
SIMILAR SPECIES Wood Blewit (p.27) has a violet cap and gills when young. *L. sordida* is more lilac-brown. St George's Mushroom (p.62) fruits earlier and lacks the lilac stem. Clouded Funnel (p.29) has a grey cap and decurrent gills.

A large fungus often growing in rings. The thick, fleshy, convex cap matures flat, often with a depressed centre and inrolled edge. It is grey-brown, darker at the centre and frequently with a white bloom. The gills are crowded, cream-coloured, adnate to slightly decurrent. The stem is paler, and thick with a swollen base. It smells strongly of turnip.

SIZE Cap 8–20 cm, stem 5–12 cm x 20–30 mm.
HABITAT In litter of broad-leaved and coniferous woods.
SEASON Autumn to early winter.
EDIBLE Can cause digestive upset so best avoided.
SIMILAR SPECIES It can be confused with Wood Blewit (p.27), which has pale-pink spores and an inrolled cap edge but with sinuate, initially lilac-coloured gills and a fruity smell.

Ampulloclitocybe (formerly Clitocybe) clavipes

The cap is initially convex with an inrolled edge but later flat and often with a spongy central umbo. It is grey-brown to tan and the stem, which has a swollen base narrowing gently towards its apex, is paler. The gills are very decurrent, uncrowded and creamy-yellow. The smell is sweet and fruity.

SIZE Cap 4–8 cm, stem 4–7 cm x 10 mm (wider at base).

HABITAT Coniferous and broad-leaved woods. Also found under bracken.

SEASON Autumn.

INEDIBLE Not worth eating, and causes nausea and hot flushes when consumed with alcohol.

SIMILAR SPECIES *C. geotropa* is paler and found in woods on chalky soils. Other species of *Clitocybe* lack the swollen stem base.

The funnel-shaped, pale creamy-brown cap has a thin, wavy margin and very decurrent, crowded creamy-white gills. The smooth cream-coloured stem is tough and only slightly enlarged at its base. It smells of new-mown hay.

SIZE Cap 4–8 cm,
stem 3–7 cm x 6–10 mm.
HABITAT In leaf litter in broad-leaved woods and on heaths.
SEASON Summer to autumn.
EDIBLE Not worthwhile.
SIMILAR SPECIES Tawny Funnel (*Lepista* – formerly *Clitocybe* – *flaccida*) is orange-brown with crowded, deeply decurrent gills. Stem base is matted with leaf litter.

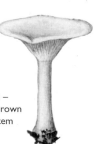

Easily identified by its strong aniseed smell
and blue-green colour. The young blue-
green cap is convex with an inrolled margin.
Older flat caps dry to pale cream with a wavy margin.
The adnate to slightly decurrent, green-tinged gills
pale with age. The stem colour is similar to the cap's,
the base is covered with white down.

SIZE Cap 3–6 cm, stem 4–8 cm x 5–10 mm.
HABITAT Woodland leaf litter, usually beech or oak.
SEASON Late summer to autumn.
EDIBLE Thin-fleshed. Best dried.
SIMILAR SPECIES *C. fragrans* also smells of aniseed but has
a smaller, yellow-brown cap, buff gills and a long, thin stem.
Blue Roundhead (p.118) has a shiny, blue-green cap with
brown gills and a ring on the scaly stem.

A very poisonous small fungus. The creamy white cap has a frosted appearance with pale ochre and flesh tones. Initially convex with an inrolled margin, the smooth cap becomes flat or slightly depressed and wavy-edged. The crowded, pale, flesh-coloured gills are shortly decurrent on to a creamy stem.

SIZE Cap 2–4 cm, stem 2–4 cm x 5–10 mm.
HABITAT Lawns and short grassland, often in rings.
SEASON Midsummer to late autumn.
POISONOUS Excessive salivation and sweating shortly after ingestion. Can be fatal.
SIMILAR SPECIES The equally deadly *C. rivulosa* is now considered the same species. The bell-shaped Fairy Ring Champignon (p.39) has widely spaced gills and a hay-like smell.

The dense woolly hairs at the stem base inspire the descriptive common name and cling to dead leaves. The thin, leathery, flat cap is red-brown to pale yellow as are the spaced adnexed/free gills. The lower half of the slender stem is covered with yellow or pale brown woolly hairs.

SIZE Cap 3–6 cm, stem 4–8 cm x 4–6 mm.

HABITAT Leaf litter of broad-leaved woods. Occasionally among coniferous needle litter.

SEASON Late summer to autumn.

INEDIBLE It has a peppery taste. Sometimes used to add spice to certain dishes.

SIMILAR SPECIES Clustered Toughshank (p.36) grows in compact tufts. The pale cap bears more crowded gills. Velvety stem.

Living up to its name with a russet-brown, smooth hollow fibrous stem that is slightly swollen at the base. The thin, flat, dry cap is initially also russet but fades to pale buff. The very crowded, adnexed/free gills are creamy-white, sometimes pale yellow. Mushroom-like smell.

SIZE Cap 2–5 cm, stem 3–6 cm x 2–4 mm.
HABITAT Gregarious among leaf litter in broad-leaved woods. Also under bracken on heaths.
SEASON Midsummer to late autumn.
INEDIBLE Tough. Poisonous if eaten raw.
SIMILAR SPECIES The similar-coloured Spindle Toughshank (*C. fusipes*) has twisted, flattened stems swollen at the middle and fusing with others at the base. On or near oak and beech stumps.

Growing in dense clumps with thin stems joined at the base, the thin, flesh-brown convex caps mature flat and dry creamy-white. The slender pink-brown, frequently flattened hollow stem is usually darker than the cap and covered with tiny grey-white down. The gills are flesh-coloured, adnexed and very crowded.

SIZE Cap 2–5 cm, stem 6–10 cm x 3–5 mm.
HABITAT Among leaf litter in broad-leaved woods, mostly with beech and often in rings.
SEASON Late summer to late autumn.
INEDIBLE Tough and not worth eating.
SIMILAR SPECIES Clustered Bonnet (p.44) has more delicate, less flat caps and grows on oak stumps. Funnels (pp. 31–33) grow in similar habitats but have decurrent gills.

Also known as Greasy Toughshank. The fleshy cap has a distinctive greasy or buttery feel, especially on the cap's umbo. This retains the date-brown colour that on most older caps dries pale buff. It has cream-coloured, crowded adnexed gills. The stem tapers from a much thicker base where it has fine white hairs.

SIZE Cap 4–8 cm, stem 5–9 cm x 10 mm (average).

HABITAT Among broad-leaved tree litter and coniferous needle litter, often in troops and rings.

SEASON Early autumn to early winter.

EDIBLE Not worthwhile.

SIMILAR SPECIES The less common *C. distorta* is red-brown, lacks the greasy feel and swollen stem base. Usually with oak or birch.

Spotted Toughshank

TRICHOLOMATACEAE FAMILY

Collybia maculata

This large, thick-fleshed, initially white species develops rusty-brown spots on its cap, gills and stem. Handling also causes browning. The deeply convex cap matures flat but often misshapen. The white gills are thin, adnexed and very crowded. The tall, broad, fibrous stem continues root-like underground.

SIZE Cap 6–12 cm, stem 8–12 cm x 8–15 mm.
HABITAT Under trees. Usually with birch and pine. Also on heaths with bracken.
SEASON Midsummer to late autumn.
INEDIBLE Very tough with a bitter taste.
SIMILAR SPECIES A similar-sized fungus that is also white but with blue spots is *Tricholoma columbetta*, although this has sinuate gills.

This causes rings of dead grass in lawns. The small, tan, bell-shaped caps retain an umbo in old specimens, which dry dirty-white. The wavy margins are often grooved when wet. The adnexed/free cream gills are well spaced but have intermediates near the edge. The straw-coloured stem is tough and pliable. Smells of new-mown hay.

SIZE Cap 2–5 cm, stem 3–6 cm x 2–4 mm.
HABITAT Short grass in lawns/pastures.
SEASON Early summer to late autumn.
EDIBLE Use dried in soups and stews. Beware confusion with poisonous species (see below).
SIMILAR SPECIES Often found growing with the poisonous Ivory Funnel (p.33), which lacks the grooved cap edge, has more crowded gills and a brittle stem.

This tiny, very beautiful fungus is tougher than it looks. The thin, creamy-white cap is radially furrowed like a parachute, from the darker, central depressed region to the scalloped margin. The cream, widely spaced gills are not attached to the stem but to a collar round its apex, like the spokes from a wheel hub. The long red-brown, wiry stem is darker at the base.

SIZE Cap 0.7–1.3 cm, stem 2–4 cm x 1–2 mm.
HABITAT On dead twigs, bark and occasionally leaf litter of broad-leaved trees.
SEASON Midsummer to late autumn.
INEDIBLE It is tough and very small.
SIMILAR SPECIES Horsehair Parachute (p.41) has a pinky-brown cap and more crowded gills attached to the stem. *M. epiphyllus* is white with a pale stem but no collar.

The dark-brown to black, thin, wiry stem is very like horse's hair. The convex cap is radially furrowed from a dark red-brown, slightly depressed central region; the rest is dull flesh-pink. The pinky-brown gills are adnately attached. The black stem is smooth, shiny and tough.

SIZE Cap 0.5–1 cm, stem 3–5 cm x 1 mm.
HABITAT In large numbers on dead needles and twigs of coniferous trees. Also on dead leaves and stems of heather.
SEASON Spring to early winter.
INEDIBLE Tough and insubstantial.
SIMILAR SPECIES *Marasmiellus ramealis* is pinky-white with a much shorter, broader, often curved, scurfy stem. Most frequent on dead blackberry stems.

The bell-shaped cap is light brown to grey, paler at the margin which is furrowed and later upturned. It flattens and wrinkles with age but retains a central umbo. The gills are pale grey with a flesh tint, adnate and spaced with cross veins. The stem is smooth, often curved, the same colour as the cap, with white hairs at its base. It smells of meal. Formerly known as Bonnet Bell Cap.

SIZE Cap 2–6 cm, stem 3–8 cm x 2–5 mm.
HABITAT Clustered on broad-leaved stumps and fallen logs.
SEASON Most of the year.
EDIBLE Insubstantial and not worth eating.
SIMILAR SPECIES Conifer Bonnet (p.43) is more densely tufted, has an ammonia-like smell and is associated with coniferous trees.

One of a number of Bonnets with a distinctive smell of ammonia. The small, browny-grey, bell-shaped cap often has an olive tint. The margin is paler when wet, showing darker lines. The adnate gills ascend to the stem apex and are pale grey with a white margin. The thin, smooth stem is cap-coloured.

SIZE Cap 1–3 cm, stem 4–6 cm x 2 mm.
HABITAT In tufts on coniferous stumps; twigs and logs.
SEASON Late summer to autumn.
INEDIBLE Not worth eating despite its mild taste.
SIMILAR SPECIES *M. leptocephala* has a comparable smell but is less robust, rarely clustered and occurs on decaying wood and among leaf or needle litter.

As its name suggests, this grows in tufts. It is red-brown with a darker central umbo and a striate margin that extends beyond the white, adnate gills, which mature flesh-pink. The long, frequently twisted stem is off-white at the apex but more yellow-brown in the centre and dark red-brown at the base, which is covered with white, woolly hairs. It smells of rancid oil.

SIZE Cap 2–3 cm, stem 4–10 cm x 2–3 mm.
HABITAT Densely tufted. Commonest on oak stumps and logs.
SEASON Late summer to autumn.
INEDIBLE Not worth eating despite the mild taste.
SIMILAR SPECIES On stumps – Common Bonnet (p.42) lacks a dark stem base. *M. haematopus* has red-brown caps and stems that exude a red latex when damaged.

The common name refers to the milky-white latex that is exuded from the broken stems of young specimens. The conical cap has a brown central umbo; the remainder is paler and striated. (In var. *candida* the whole fruitbody is white.) It has adnate, ascending, grey-white gills. The stem is grey, darker at the base. It smells faintly of radish.

SIZE Cap 1–2 cm, stem 4–6 cm x 1–2 mm.

HABITAT Among leaf and needle litter of both broad-leaved and coniferous trees.

SEASON Late summer to late autumn.

EDIBLE Not worth eating.

SIMILAR SPECIES The less common var. *nigra* also exudes a white juice from its broken stem but the cap and stem apex is a deeper brown-black colour. On acid soils and burnt ground.

The conical cap later flattens but maintains a dark red-brown central umbo. The rest is pinky-brown with darker striations. The adnate pinky-white gills have a red-brown margin. The hollow, long, russet stem exudes a pink-red latex when broken.

SIZE Cap 0.5–1.5 cm, stem 4–7 cm x 1 mm.
HABITAT Conifer woods on needles and moss-covered wood. Also on heathland.
SEASON Summer to autumn.
EDIBLE Not worthwhile.
SIMILAR SPECIES The larger *M. haematopus* has a stem that exudes a darker red latex when damaged and grows clustered on rotting broad-leaved wood.

It has quite a large cap (for a Bonnet) that becomes flat or even slightly depressed around its central umbo. The margin is lined when moist. The cap and stem have a violet or purple hue. The adnate to almost decurrent, crowded gills are pale grey with a lilac tint and the stem is smooth and thick. It smells strongly of radish.

SIZE Cap 2–5 cm, stem 3–8 cm x 3–8 mm.
HABITAT Among leaf litter in both broad-leaved and coniferous woodland.
SEASON Summer to late autumn.
POISONOUS Contains muscarine.
SIMILAR SPECIES The larger pink *M. rosea* is mostly found in southern woods on chalk. The edible Amethyst Deceiver (p.26) has widely spaced violet gills.

Yellowleg Bonnet

TRICHOLOMATACEAE FAMILY

Mycena epipterygia

The yellow stems of this species make it stand out despite its small size. The convex yellow-brown cap is semi-transparent with striations almost to its centre. Its smooth surface is slimy when moist. The white gills are adnate to slightly decurrent. The long slender stem is a bright lemon-yellow and sticky to the touch.

SIZE Cap 1–2 cm, stem 4–8 cm x 1–3 mm.

HABITAT In coniferous and broad-leaved woods among moss, grass and leaf litter. Also on heaths.

SEASON Late summer to autumn.

EDIBLE Too small to be worth eating.

SIMILAR SPECIES Other yellow-stemmed Bell Caps include *M. epipterygioides*. This grows on wood, including stumps; mostly on conifers.

This minute species is distinguished by its bright orange colour. The tiny, convex, orange cap is more yellow at the striate, semi-transparent margin. The pale-yellow gills ascend to the top of the yellow, thread-like stem, which is whiter at the base.

SIZE Cap 0.4–1 cm,
stem 3–4 cm x 0.5–1 mm.
HABITAT On rich woodland soil often associated with dog's mercury.
SEASON Summer to autumn.
INEDIBLE Insubstantial.

SIMILAR SPECIES
The tiny *M. adonis* also grows in moss but has a pink cap and gills. The larger *M. flavoalba* is yellow with decurrent gills and grows on old lawns. *M. acicula* is easily confused with Orange Mosscap (p.50) but this has very decurrent gills.

This delicate white-spored fungus was previously included with the Bonnets from which it differs in having deeply decurrent gills. The convex cap flattens with age but has a centrally depressed region which is a darker orange. The margin is grooved and often wavy-edged. The pale orange, decurrent gills descend on to the yellow-orange stem which narrows to its base.

SIZE Cap 0.4–1 cm, stem 3–6 cm x 1 mm.
HABITAT Among moss in grassland, heathland and woodland.
SEASON Summer to autumn.
INEDIBLE Too small to be worth eating.
SIMILAR SPECIES The larger grey-brown *R. swartzii* is always associated with mosses. Orange Bonnet (p.49) is not funnel-shaped.

A common little fungus of moors and heaths, formerly known as *Omphalina ericetorum*. The yellow-brown convex cap has a darker, centrally depressed area surrounded by a deeply grooved, inrolled margin – hence the Navel in its name. Some of the widely spaced, decurrent, pale-ochre gills are forked. It has a smooth, pale-brown stem. Commonest in the north and west.

SIZE Cap 1–2 cm, stem 1–3 cm x 2–3 mm.
HABITAT On acid peaty soil among moss or lichens. Also on rotten wood.
SEASON Early summer to late autumn.
INEDIBLE Insubstantial.
SIMILAR SPECIES *Omphalina pyxidata* is red-brown with more crowded gills and grows on burnt soil or in short grass.

Xerula radicata (formerly *Oudemansiella radicata*)

The convex red-brown cap matures flat with a broad central umbo around which the surface is radially wrinkled. It is slimy when wet, shiny when dry. The white gills are broad and adnexed. The long, longitudinally grooved, tough stem is paler than the cap. It is darker and broader at the base before narrowing and continuing underground like a root.

SIZE Cap 4–10 cm, stem 8–20 cm x 5–10 mm.
HABITAT Arising from roots and buried wood of broad-leaved trees, especially beech. Singly or in small groups.
SEASON Midsummer to autumn.
INEDIBLE Not worth eating due to slimy cap.
SIMILAR SPECIES The less common *X. pudens* has a dry, grey-brown, felty cap and a stem covered with red-brown velvety hairs.

Also known as the Poached Egg Fungus. A beautiful fungus with a shiny, semi-transparent, porcelain-like appearance. The broadly convex, creamy-grey cap is wrinkled at the margin and very slimy when moist. It has broad, spaced, adnate cream-coloured gills. The stem is white above the large ring; the lower part is greyer, sticky and often bent to bring the cap to the horizontal.

SIZE Cap 4–8 cm, stem 4–8 cm x 3–7 mm.

HABITAT Typically on beech; stumps, logs and as a weak parasite on trunks and side branches of mature living trees. Usually clustered.

SEASON Late summer to early winter.

EDIBLE The slime must be removed first.

SIMILAR SPECIES None.

Flammulina velutipes

This species continues fruiting through the winter. The medium-sized caps soon flatten and are a distinctive orange-brown, darker at the centre, slightly lined at the margin. The surface is shiny and sticky. The adnate, broad, spaced, white gills mature pale yellow. The stem is tough, velvety, cap-coloured at the apex and dark brown at the base.

SIZE Cap 2–7 cm, stem 3–10 cm x 3–8 mm.
HABITAT Clustered on dead wood (stumps, logs and standing timber) of many broad-leaved trees, especially elm.
SEASON Autumn to spring.
EDIBLE Remove the slimy layer and tough stem.
SIMILAR SPECIES Confusable with other tufted wood rotters such as Sheathed Woodtuft (p.115) and Sulphur Tuft (p.116) but these have brown spores and a ringed stem.

A destructive species, it kills a wide range of trees and shrubs and spreads to new hosts by bootlace-like strands. The deeply convex caps mature flat with tiny scales at the centre. The colour ranges from honey-yellow to red-brown. The gills are adnate to decurrent, crowded, flesh-coloured and later have rusty spots. The stem is long with a yellow-white ring; its brown base not swollen.

SIZE Cap 5–15 cm, stem 6–12 cm x 10–20 mm.
HABITAT Densely clustered on both living trunks and dead stumps and roots of broad-leaved trees and less often on conifers.
SEASON Late summer to early winter.
EDIBLE Not easily digested. Must be well cooked.
SIMILAR SPECIES A range of similar, less destructive species has recently been indentified.

Armillaria gallica

Unlike Honey Fungus (p.55), this is a weak parasite that rots dead wood. The cap is similar to Honey Fungus, with a more scaly top. The immature gills are covered with a cobweb-like veil that leaves a transient ring on the short, stocky stem, which has a noticeably swollen base.

SIZE Cap 5–15 cm, stem 4–10 cm x 20–30 mm.
HABITAT On tree stumps and dead wood, including conifers. Solitary or in small clumps and not densely clustered.
SEASON Late autumn to early winter.
EDIBLE Not easily digested. Must be well cooked.
SIMILAR SPECIES Honey Fungus (p.55) lacks the bulbous base. Shaggy Scalycap (p.113) with brown spores has upturned brown scales on its cap and at the stem base.

Smells of soap. The thick-fleshed, broadly convex cap has an incurved edge and ranges from olive to grey-brown but may be much paler at the margin. The smooth cap cracks when dry and is pink where damaged. It has broad, spaced, sinuate, cream to pale-green gills. The cream stem often has grey-brown fibres or scales. It tapers to a root-like base.

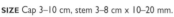

SIZE Cap 3–10 cm, stem 3–8 cm x 10–20 mm.
HABITAT In troops, usually under trees.
SEASON Midsummer to autumn.
INEDIBLE Bitter taste. May cause digestive upset and easily confused with poisonous species.
SIMILAR SPECIES *T. ustale* has a sticky, chestnut-brown cap, no soapy smell and is found in broad-leaved woods. Usually with beech.

Grey Knight

Tricholoma terreum

The cap is initially bell-shaped and finally almost flat with a broad umbo. It is dark grey to black with radiating fibrils and an inrolled margin. The gills are broad, spaced, sinuate and grey-white. The stem is pale grey, smooth and cylindrical.

SIZE Cap 4–8 cm, stem 3–7 cm x 10 mm.
HABITAT On soil under pine trees.
SEASON Late summer to autumn.
EDIBLE Has a mild taste but other grey species of *Tricholoma* are poisonous.
SIMILAR SPECIES *T. virgatum*, which grows on soil in broad-leaved woodland, is of a similar size and also has grey-brown fibrils on the cap but the centre is markedly umbonate, the stem has a slightly swollen base and the flesh has a bitter, burning taste.

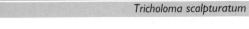

The cap is initially grey-brown and convex, maturing pale beige and flat but with scales at the centre and a wavy incurled margin which is covered with radiating fibres. Smells of flour and yellows from the margin when old or picked. The grey-white, broad, sinuate gills also yellow with age. The stem is cylindrical and often bent. Also known incorrectly as *T. argyraceum*.

SIZE Cap 3–7 cm x 3–6 cm x 5–10 mm.
HABITAT Mostly under beech. Also with birch on heathland.
SEASON Late summer to late autumn.
EDIBLE A mild taste but not very good eating.
SIMILAR SPECIES Grey Knight (p.58) does not yellow, and lacks both scales and smell.

Birch Knight

TRICHOLOMATACEAE FAMILY

Tricholoma fulvum

The orange-brown cap flattens but for a broad, darker, central umbo and a faintly ribbed margin. The surface is smooth, shiny and sticky when young. The broad, sinuate, yellow-brown gills often have darker spots. The stem apex is paler than the cap but darker at the stem base and covered with red-brown fibres. It is sticky when moist and has an unpleasant mealy smell.

SIZE Cap 5–10 cm, stem 7–11 cm x 10–15 mm.
HABITAT On wet, acidic soils mostly under birch. Also with beech and oak.
SEASON Autumn.
EDIBLE Poor. Can be confused with other brown species.
SIMILAR SPECIES *T. ustale* has a sticky brown cap that dries shiny. It has rust-spotted gills and a similar habitat.

A number of woodland fungi have a yellow cap, stem and gills but this is the only one to smell strongly of coal-gas. The sulphur-yellow, matt cap surface often includes red-brown tints. It has similar-coloured broad, distant, sinuate gills. The yellow stem is covered with small, red-brown fibrils.

SIZE Cap 3–8 cm, stem 3–8 cm x 8–18 mm.
HABITAT Under broad-leaved trees, e.g. oak or beech. In grassland with rockrose.
SEASON Autumn.
INEDIBLE The smell is unpleasant.
SIMILAR SPECIES *T. equestre* (previously *flavovirens*) is also yellow but has brown scales on its umbo. Yellow species of Webcap have adnate gills, brown spores and a cobweb veil when young (see p.121).

St George's Mushroom

TRICHOLOMATACEAE FAMILY

Calocybe gambosa (Tricholoma gambosum)

So called because it fruits as early as 23 April, though it is most frequent in May. The mealy-smelling, fleshy cap starts domed with inrolled edges but becomes flatter with wavy, often split margins. It is dry, smooth, creamy-white to pale tan. The white, sinuate gills are very crowded. The broad, solid, white stem is often curved and thicker at the base.

SIZE Cap 5–12 cm, stem 4–10 cm x 20–40 mm.

HABITAT In pastures, road verges and lawns. Also among spring flowers in woodland edges and hedgerows.

SEASON April to June.

EDIBLE Good when young; with a firm, dry flesh.

SIMILAR SPECIES Most similar-looking species fruit later but beware the poisonous Deadly Fibrecap (p.124).

The fruitbodies are in crowded clusters. The almost hemispherical young caps age more convex with a broad central umbo where the grey to hazel-brown colour is darkest. The margin is wavy. The gills are adnate and a dirty white colour. The grey-white stem is usually flattened, bent and twisted, fusing with several others.

SIZE Cap 6–10 cm, stem 5–10 cm x 10–18 mm.

HABITAT On soil in broad-leaved woodland, gardens, parks and even pavements.

SEASON Midsummer to autumn.

EDIBLE Not highly rated. Beware highly poisonous lookalike Livid Pinkgill (see p.107).

SIMILAR SPECIES *L. connatum* has a satiny white cap with shortly decurrent gills. Common in Scotland.

Common Cavalier

TRICHOLOMATACEAE FAMILY

Melanoleuca polioleuca

The smooth cap is dark brown when moist but dries much paler.
The crowded, white gills are weakly sinuate. The stem has pale-
brown fibres on a white background and is swollen at the base.

SIZE Cap 4–10 cm, stem 4–8 cm x 10 mm.
HABITAT Among grass in pastureland and
with leaf litter in woodlands. Solitary or in
small troops.
SEASON Late summer to autumn.
EDIBLE Insipid taste, so not recommended.
SIMILAR SPECIES Common Cavalier was
formerly confused with *M. melaleuca*, which is
now considered to be rare in Britain. Deer Shield
(p.101) is easily confused with *Melanoleuca* species
but has pink spores and always grows on rotting wood.

The name refers to the colour of the cap and gills. The large, flat cap is covered with fine, red-purple scales, less dense near the incurved margins where the background yellow shows through. The apricot-yellow gills are weakly sinuate and crowded. The scaly, cap-coloured stem often curves. It has a musty smell.

SIZE Cap 4–12 cm,
stem 4–10 cm x 10–25 mm.
HABITAT On old stumps and decaying wood of conifers, mostly with pine.
SEASON Autumn.
INEDIBLE Not poisonous but not edible, despite its name.
SIMILAR SPECIES The smaller, yellower *T. decora* also grows on conifer stumps.

Formerly known as *H. nivea*, its thin-fleshed cap is initially deeply convex but expands flat with an almost transparent, lined margin that often upturns to reveal the gill edges. It is smooth to greasy, pale beige when young and moist, but drying creamy-white. The gills are the same colour as the cap, broad, well-spaced and decurrent. The stem is cylindrical and white.

SIZE Cap 2–5 cm, stem 2–5 cm x 4–8 mm.
HABITAT Among short grass in lawns, pastures and moors.
SEASON Autumn to early winter.
EDIBLE Beware confusion with poisonous species.
SIMILAR SPECIES *H. russocoriacea* smells of pencils! The poisonous Ivory Funnel (p.33) has flesh-coloured, crowded gills. Fairy Ring Champignon (p.39) has adnexed gills.

The pale-orange to lemon cap has wavy, split margins that often reveal the gill edges. The smooth, shiny, slimy surface has lined margins when moist. The gills are pale yellow with a whiter edge, moderately crowded and deeply notched where they attach to the stem. The stem is drier, grooved and often flattened.

SIZE Cap 3–6 cm, stem 5–7 cm x 5–10 mm.
HABITAT Among grass in lawns and short grass.
SEASON Midsummer to autumn.
INEDIBLE Small and slimy, with an insipid taste.
SIMILAR SPECIES Other yellow Waxcaps include *H. ceracea* with a smaller, greasy cap and crowded gills. Old Parrot Waxcaps (p.72) have thick, adnate gills.

The small, deep-orange cap soon flattens with a paler, lined margin that is often split when old. The greasy cap surface later dries and the centre breaks up into small scales. The orange-yellow gills are adnate or shortly decurrent. The stem, similar in colour, is often flattened and tapers to a thinner, paler base. It is odourless.

SIZE Cap 1–4 cm, stem 2–4 cm x 4–7 mm.
HABITAT In pasture and heathland on acid soil.
SEASON Autumn.
INEDIBLE Not recorded as being worth eating.
SIMILAR SPECIES The larger, fleshier Meadow Waxcap (p.70) is more tawny-apricot and the pointed Blackening Waxcap (p.69) darkens with age. *H. ceracea* has a yellow cap with a slightly grooved margin.

This common species blackens with age. The medium-sized, bell-shaped cap later becomes more convex. The yellow, orange or red cap is slightly greasy and covered with small, radiating fibrils. The wavy margin often splits. The broad, pale-yellow gills are almost free of the stem and have a toothed edge. The stem has a white base. The cap, gills and stem all blacken on handling and with age.

SIZE Cap 4–7 cm, stem 4–10 cm x 5–10 mm.

HABITAT In grass on pastureland, lawns and road verges.

SEASON Midsummer to autumn.

INEDIBLE Slightly bitter taste; edibility suspect.

SIMILAR SPECIES Redder specimens were previously classed as *H. nigrescens* but are now included with *H. conica*. The rarer, lilac-pink *H. calyptriformis* has a conical, lobed cap.

Hygrocybe pratensis

The fleshy convex cap becomes flat and concave but retains a broad, central umbo. The colour varies from apricot to pale tawny-buff and the greasy surface dries with age when the margin often splits. The thick, widely spaced, waxy gills are decurrent and have cross-veins. The stout, short stem narrows to its base.

SIZE Cap 3–10 cm, stem 4–8 cm x 10–15 mm.

HABITAT Short grass of lawns, pastures and woods.

SEASON Autumn to early winter.

EDIBLE Needs slow cooking. Mild taste.

SIMILAR SPECIES *H. quieta* is more orange and its gills are not decurrent. False Chanterelle (p.166) has an inrolled cap margin, crowded orange gills and a slender stem. Chanterelle (p.167) grows with moss in woods.

The small, bright, cherry-red, convex cap is smooth and shiny when young and moist, but dries and fades to orange-pink with age. The thick, orange-red gills pale with age. The attachment is adnate but with a small decurrent tooth. The cylindrical, orange-red stem tapers to a pale base where it may become flattened.

SIZE Cap 2–5 cm, stem 3–6 cm x 5–8 mm.

HABITAT Among short grass and moss in lawns and pasture.

SEASON Late summer to early winter.

EDIBLE Not poisonous despite the orange-red flesh.

SIMILAR SPECIES The much larger and fleshier *H. punicea* has adnexed gills and dark-red cap flesh. The smaller, orange-red *H. miniata* (p.68) has a dry cap, minutely scaly near the centre.

Parrot Waxcap

Hygrocybe psittacina

The bell-shaped cap has a lined margin and is very slimy. Older caps dry, flatten and lose their green colour, becoming yellow or even pink-tinged. The thick, adnate gills start green but age yellow from their margins. The slimy stem is initially green near the apex and yellow at the broader base but the green disappears with age. It is odourless.

SIZE Cap 2–4 cm, stem 4–6 cm x 4–8 mm.
HABITAT Among grass in poor pasture and open woodland.
SEASON Midsummer to late autumn.
INEDIBLE Not poisonous but not pleasant to eat.
SIMILAR SPECIES Older specimens are like the orange and yellow Waxcaps but these lack green tints. Blue Roundhead (p.118) is more blue-green and has purple-black spores.

Most fungi stop fruiting in late autumn but this occasional species does not appear until the frosts start, as its name suggests. Convex when young, flat later, the olive-brown, slimy cap dries pale ochre. The margin remains inrolled until old. The broad, shortly decurrent, creamy gills mature pale orange. The young stem has a ring-like zone and is white and slimy; drying and ageing pale orange. It is odourless.

SIZE Cap 3–5 cm, stem 5–7 cm x 5–10 mm.
HABITAT Among needle litter in coniferous or mixed woods, usually with pine.
SEASON Late autumn to early winter.
EDIBLE Mild tasting but poor texture.
SIMILAR SPECIES *H. agathosmus* has a grey cap, cream gills and smells of almonds.

Brittlegills are unusual in that they can be readily crumbled. In this, the commonest of the yellow species, the convex cap soon flattens and may become concave. The matt, ochre-yellow, peelable skin matures with a faintly grooved edge. The pale-cream gills are neat, adnate and quite crowded. The white, cylindrical stem greys with age. The taste is acrid.

SIZE Cap 4–10 cm, stem 4–8 cm x 10–20 mm.

HABITAT In both broad-leaved and coniferous woods.

SEASON Late summer to early winter.

EDIBLE Peppery flesh is not to everyone's taste.

SIMILAR SPECIES Both Golden Brittlegill (p.75) and Geranium Brittlegill (p.77) have yellow gills. The Yellow Swamp Brittlegill (p.76) is bright yellow and grows with birch on wet ground.

Distinguished from Ochre Brittlegill (p.74) by its usually smaller, thin-fleshed, more convex cap, which is golden or egg-yolk yellow. The brittle, white stem is slightly broader at the base. The crowded adnate gills are a rich orange-yellow. Older specimens smell of apricots. Formerly known as *R. lutea*.

SIZE Cap 2–6 cm, stem 2–6 cm x 6–12 mm.
HABITAT Under broad-leaved trees, especially oak, birch or beech.
SEASON Late summer to autumn.
EDIBLE Mild tasting but rather insubstantial.
SIMILAR SPECIES The larger Geranium Brittlegill (p.77) has pale-yellow gills and is distinguished by its darker cap, off-white stem, burning taste and geranium smell.

Yellow Swamp Brittlegill

RUSSULACEAE FAMILY

Russula claroflava

Best identified by its habitat, as it is confined to very wet ground under birch. The fleshy, bright-yellow cap remains convex with a shiny, slightly sticky surface. The pale, ochre-yellow, adnexed gills are quite crowded. The stem is white and cylindrical. The gills and other parts bruise dark grey. It has a pleasant smell.

SIZE Cap 4–10 cm, stem 5–10 cm x 10–20 mm.
HABITAT In wet ground under birch trees; often with *Sphagnum* (bog) moss.
SEASON Summer to autumn.
EDIBLE Has a pleasant texture and taste.
SIMILAR SPECIES No other Brittlegill has a clear yellow cap and such a specific habitat.

This species is distinguished from Ochre Brittlegill (p.74), which has a similar-coloured cap, by the fact that the yellow-brown cap colour is also found (slightly paler) on the gills and stem. The cap, initially sticky and convex, soon flattens and may become concave. It only peels at the margin, which is slightly furrowed. The gills are crowded, adnexed and straw-coloured, as is the cylindrical stem. It smells of geranium or cooked fruit.

SIZE Cap 4–10 cm, stem 3–8 cm x 10–20 mm.
HABITAT Most frequent under beech trees.
SEASON Autumn.
INEDIBLE The flesh has a very hot taste.
SIMILAR SPECIES The mild-tasting Golden Brittlegill (p.75) has a white stem.

This large, honey-brown *Russula* has a slimy feel to its cap, which is distinctly furrowed and warty at the margin, and which often matures wavy and split. The thick, spaced, adnate gills are dirty cream as is the hollow, frequently flattened stem. Both gills and stem age brown-spotted. It has an unpleasant oily smell, like rancid butter.

SIZE Cap 6–15 cm, stem 6–15 cm x 20–40 mm.
HABITAT Under broad-leaved trees, usually with beech or oak.
SEASON Summer to autumn.
INEDIBLE Unpleasant smell and peppery cap flesh.
SIMILAR SPECIES The smaller *R. subfoetens* has a similarly coloured, grooved, sticky cap but with an unpleasant smell and flesh that yellows on cutting.

While all Brittlegills are crumbly this small species is especially delicate, as its name implies. The thin-fleshed, flat cap is often depressed at the centre where it is a darker purple in contrast to the more violet or pink margin, which is usually grooved. The pale-cream, adnate gills have toothed edges (visible only through a lens). The white stem is tinged with yellow and is swollen at the base. It smells of boiled sweets (pear drops).

SIZE Cap 2–6 cm, stem 3–6 cm x 5–10 mm.
HABITAT Usually under birches but also with beech or oak.
SEASON Late summer to autumn.
INEDIBLE Has a very acrid taste.
SIMILAR SPECIES Birch Brittlegill (p.80) is more yellow-pink, has more widely spaced white gills and lacks the fruity smell.

Birch Brittlegill

Russula betularum

This small, thin-fleshed *Russula* is always found near birch. The convex to flat cap is pale red-pink with areas of yellow-buff. The furrowed margin is frequently warty. The entire skin can be peeled. The gills are adnexed, white and with a slightly toothed edge. The white stem is often longer than the cap diameter. The smell is faintly fruity.

SIZE Cap 2–6 cm, stem 3–7 cm x 5–8 mm
HABITAT Always associated with birches, often in moss.
SEASON Late summer to autumn.
INEDIBLE Very acrid taste.
SIMILAR SPECIES Other pink-red species are not restricted to birch and include Fragile Brittlegill (p.79) and The Flirt (p.81).

Old specimens live up to their names, as the skin peels and pulls away from the cap margin, revealing the tooth-like white flesh and gill tops. The cap colour varies from pinky-red to pale brown and often includes olive tints. The margin is shallowly furrowed. The adnexed, crowded, pale-cream gills often fork near the stem and later discolour with rusty spots. The white, firm stem narrows at its base.

SIZE Cap 5–10 cm, stem 4–10 cm x 10–25 mm.
HABITAT Mostly with oak, also under beech or birch.
SEASON Midsummer to early autumn.
EDIBLE Pleasant nutty taste.
SIMILAR SPECIES *R. nitida* has a similar-coloured cap with a peeling margin but pale-yellow gills. Wet ground under birch.

A very common species with a firm fleshy cap that is predominantly a mix of blue and yellow but often includes violet, grey, brown and green tints; like the many colours of a charcoal flame. The crowded, white gills are adnexed, often forked and unusually pliable for a *Russula*. The solid, white stem may show purple tints. The smell is indistinct. Charcoal Burner is much less crumbly than other Brittlegills.

SIZE Cap 5–15 cm, stem 5–10 cm x 10–30 mm.
HABITAT Usually with beech or oak but also found with birch and sweet chestnut.
SEASON Summer to late autumn.
EDIBLE Mild taste and firm texture.
SIMILAR SPECIES *R. parazurea* has a grey-blue, scurfy cap and cream-coloured gills.

This has the crumbly texture typical of a *Russula* but with a smooth, firm cap that starts convex but matures flatter with a central depression. A shiny, red-purple margin surrounds the dark purple to black centre. The gills are white, adnate and quite crowded. The white stem becomes streaked with grey and the base discolours pinky-brown. It smells faintly of apples.

SIZE Cap 4–12 cm, stem 3–6 cm x 10–20 mm.
HABITAT Broad-leaved woodland, with oak.
Also with beech and birch.
SEASON Summer to autumn.
EDIBLE Must be cooked. Mild to slightly peppery.
SIMILAR SPECIES Some forms of Crab Brittlegill
(p.87) have a dark-purple cap but the gills are
straw-coloured.

Blackening Brittlegill

Russula nigricans

This species varies considerably in shape, size and colour as it matures. The cap is initially small, dirty-white, deeply convex and with an inrolled margin; as it flattens it turns brown and finally large, concave and black. Cracks reveal the paler flesh below. The well-spaced, adnate gills are very thick and start creamy-yellow but become spotted with red-brown and later turn black. The firm stem also darkens with age. White flesh ages red then black.

SIZE Cap 8–25 cm, stem 4–10 cm x 15–30 mm.
HABITAT All kinds of woodland but commonly with beech or oak.
SEASON Midsummer to early winter.
EDIBLE Good when young, later tough and full of maggots.
SIMILAR SPECIES *R. densifolia* has crowded, decurrent gills.

The best known of the *Russula* species because of its reputation for causing sickness. The convex cap, which soon flattens, is thin-fleshed and easily broken. It is shiny and sticky when wet, with easily peelable skin that is a brilliant cherry-red with some paler areas. The creamy-white, adnexed gills are moderately spaced. The spongy, white stem is swollen at the base. It has a slightly fruity smell.

SIZE Cap 5–10 cm, stem 4–8 cm x 15–20 mm.

HABITAT Under conifers on moist, acid soil, often with moss.

SEASON Midsummer to autumn.

POISONOUS The acrid flesh causes vomiting.

SIMILAR SPECIES Beechwood Sickener (p.86).

Beechwood Sickener

Russula nobilis (formerly mairei)

Unlike the Sickener (p.85), this species has a smaller, firmer, matt cap that is a lighter shade of scarlet and occasionally pink or almost white. The crowded, white gills age slightly grey-green. The firm, solid stem yellows but does not swell at the base. It smells of coconut when young, sweeter when old.

SIZE Cap 3–7 cm, stem 2–5 cm x 10–15 mm.
HABITAT Under beech trees.
SEASON Autumn.
POISONOUS The acrid flesh causes sickness.
SIMILAR SPECIES Sickener (p.85) has a larger, more fragile, deep-red cap and grows under conifers. Other red species of *Russula* are paler or have off-white gills and/or stems.

As the pictures show, this species can be found in a number of different-coloured varieties. The broadly convex, smooth cap may be red or purple or wine-coloured or a mixture of all these colours. The thick, adnexed gills are pale ochre and show cross veins at their bases. The white stem has a faint pink flush and browns towards its base and with handling. Old specimens smell strongly of crab.

SIZE Cap 7–15 cm, stem 4–10 cm x 15–30 mm.
HABITAT In woodland, especially with pine.
SEASON Late summer to early winter.
EDIBLE Mild taste despite the crab-like smell.
SIMILAR SPECIES The smell of *R. xerampelina* distinguishes it from other common, similar-coloured species of *Russula*.

The pale yellow-green cap has brown tints and a darker centre. The margin is usually grooved. The adnexed, crowded, pale-ochre gills often fork. The white stem narrows at the base. It has no distinctive smell.

SIZE Cap 5–10 cm, stem 5–8 cm x 8–15 mm.
HABITAT Usually under birch or oak.
SEASON Summer to early autumn.
POISONOUS May cause digestive upset.
SIMILAR SPECIES Other green species include *R. heterophylla* with crowded, white, decurrent gills that fork near the stem; *R. virescens* (Greencracked Brittlegill) with a dry skin which cracks into a mosaic pattern; and green varieties of Charcoal Burner (p.82), which are normally dark green with shades of purple and bronze.

The woodland Milkcaps have a crumbly texture but differ from
the Brittlegills (pp.74–88) in having decurrent gills that exude a
latex (milk) when broken. Peppery Milkcap has an ivory-white,
matt, funnel-shaped cap with an inrolled margin. The very crowded,
cream-coloured, thin, decurrent gills age pinky-yellow and exude
an acrid milk when damaged. The stem is long and white.

SIZE Cap 8–15 cm, stem 4–8 cm x 20–30 mm.
HABITAT Mostly found under beech or oak.
SEASON Late summer to late autumn.
EDIBLE Dried specimens have been used as a seasoning
but the very acrid taste is not for the faint hearted.
SIMILAR SPECIES The larger Fleecy Milkcap (p.90) has
a downy cap and thick, white gills that exude copious
amounts of acrid-tasting milk.

The convex cap soon flattens and the central depression gives it a shallow funnel-shape. The creamy-white surface is velvety, especially near the inrolled margin. Older caps, up to the size of a dinner plate, have discoloured yellow or brown areas. The white, decurrent, distant gills exude lots of white milk when damaged. Older gills brown slightly. The stem is solid, white and stocky.

SIZE Cap 10–25 cm, stem 4–10 cm x 20–40 mm.
HABITAT With birch, hazel, beech and oak.
SEASON Late summer to early winter.
INEDIBLE Acrid taste when young, poor texture.
SIMILAR SPECIES Peppery Milkcap (p.89) has a long stem, smooth cap and crowded gills. *L. controversus* has flesh-coloured gills and grows with willows and poplars.

This very common species smells of bedbugs – rather oily! The broadly convex dry cap is centrally depressed when old and a dull, red-brown colour with faint, concentric, darker bands. The shortly decurrent, creamy-brown, crowded gills age darker brown and exude a creamy-white milk. The slender stem is the same colour as the cap but darker near its base.

SIZE Cap 4–9 cm, stem 4–10 cm x 6–12 mm.
HABITAT Only found in the vicinity of oak trees.
SEASON Autumn.
INEDIBLE Slight bitter taste, unpleasant smell.
SIMILAR SPECIES Beech Milkcap (p.92) grows with beech. Birch Milkcap (p.96) is smaller, lacks the cap zonation and is most common under birch.

This species is commonly found in beech woods. The depressed cap is a strange mix of grey, olive and brown with concentric bands of darker spots. It is shiny and very slimy when moist. The shortly decurrent gills start cream but grey with age and on damage because the white milk dries grey. The stem is paler than the cap and slimy when young. There is no obvious smell.

SIZE Cap 5–10 cm, stem 4–5 cm x 10–15 mm.

HABITAT Under broad-leaved trees, usually with beech.

SEASON Late summer to autumn.

INEDIBLE Slimy cap surface and very acrid taste.

SIMILAR SPECIES The much larger, slimy-capped Ugly Milkcap (p.93) is darker and typically grows under birch trees.

Once called *L. plumbeus* due to its leaden colour, this large fungus has young convex caps that are olive-brown with a felty, inrolled margin; the mature caps are dark brown to black, and flat or slightly depressed. It is sticky when moist. The shortly decurrent, creamy-buff, crowded gills are spotted with brown when old. They exude an abundant, acrid, white milk. The stocky stem is the same colour as the cap, often with shallow pits.

SIZE Cap 7–20 cm, stem 4–6 cm x 20–30 mm.
HABITAT Under birch, often among leaf litter or grass. Also with spruce and larch.
SEASON Late summer to autumn.
INEDIBLE Not recommended due to its bitter taste.
SIMILAR SPECIES Beech Milkcap (p.92). Mostly with beech.

The cap is deep red-brown, dry and slightly rough, flat or shallowly depressed but with a central pimple. The gills are shortly decurrent, crowded, pale creamy-yellow, ageing to the same colour as the stem, which is similar to that of the cap but paler. Damaged gills exude a white milk.

SIZE Cap 4–10 cm, stem 4–8 cm x 6–12 mm.

HABITAT In conifer plantations and mixed woodlands of birch and conifers.

SEASON Summer to late autumn.

INEDIBLE The initially mild-tasting milk becomes very acrid after about a minute.

SIMILAR SPECIES Curry Milkcap (*L. camphoratus*), similar in shape and colour but only half the size with watery, white milk. *L. hepaticus* is dull red-brown with browny-red spotted gills and a white milk that dries yellow.

Medium-sized, it is rich red-brown when young but paler with age. The depressed centre remains darker. The crowded gills are only shortly decurrent and mature from cream to pinky-buff. The slender stem is a similar colour to the cap near its base but much paler at its apex. Damaged gills release lots of white milk that does not dry yellow (test on a tissue).

SIZE Cap 3–8 cm, stem 4–8 cm x 4–8 mm.
HABITAT Commonest under beech, also with oak and birch.
SEASON Late summer to autumn.
INEDIBLE The milk initially tastes sweet but has a very bitter aftertaste.
SIMILAR SPECIES Birch Milkcap (p.96) is more common under birch and has an orange-brown cap with a central pimple and white milk that dries yellow.

Birch Milkcap

RUSSULACEAE FAMILY

Lactarius tabidus

The small, orange-brown cap soon flattens but usually has a central pimple and is often wrinkled near the middle. The shortly decurrent, yellow-brown, crowded gills release only small amounts of white milk when damaged. This dries yellow on a tissue. The stem narrows from its darker-coloured base to the apex.

SIZE Cap 2–4 cm, stem 2–5 cm x 4–8 mm.
HABITAT With broad-leaved trees and most common under birch in wet places, often among *Sphagnum* (bog) moss.
SEASON Midsummer to autumn.
INEDIBLE Insubstantial, with a slightly acrid taste.
SIMILAR SPECIES The darker-coloured Mild Milkcap (p.95) produces more plentiful milk, which does not dry yellow.

A small Milkcap easily identified by its smell of dried coconut.
The cap colour varies from grey-lilac to pinky-brown. It has a dry,
downy texture, thin flesh and an incurled margin when young. The
crowded, decurrent gills are flesh-coloured and produce small
amounts of white milk when damaged. The stem is paler than the
cap, becoming hollow and fragile with age.

SIZE Cap 2–5 cm, stem 3–6 cm x 4–8 mm.
HABITAT On acid soil with birch.
SEASON Late summer to late autumn.
EDIBLE Used for flavouring but has a fairly
hot taste.
SIMILAR SPECIES The larger Grey Milkcap (*L. vietus*)
has a sticky cap and a milk that dries grey on the gills;
these bruise pale brown. In moss under birch.

This species causes griping pains if eaten without careful preparation. The cap is markedly funnel-shaped when fully grown, sticky at the centre when moist and with an inrolled margin that in young specimens has a texture of lambswool. The flesh-pink cap is marked with concentric, darker-pink rings. The gills are pink, crowded and weakly decurrent. They exude a white milk. The pale-pink, solid stem matures hollow with some surface pits.

SIZE Cap 6–12 cm, stem 6–10 cm x 10–20 mm.
HABITAT Always with birch.
SEASON Late summer to autumn.
POISONOUS Parboiled it is eatable but not edible.
SIMILAR SPECIES *L. pubescens* has a paler, non-zoned cap. It also grows under birch.

This beautiful fungus is occasional in Britain. Its large, funnel-shaped cap has an inrolled margin when young and is slightly sticky. It is cream to pinky-orange with concentric bands of deep orange and faint green patches when old. The bright-orange gills are shortly decurrent, crowded and produce a carrot-coloured milk. The stocky, hollow stem is marked on the surface with orange pits near its base.

SIZE Cap 5–15 cm, stem 4–8 cm x 15–20 mm.
HABITAT Only found close to pine trees.
SEASON Late summer to autumn.
EDIBLE Best blanched before being fried.
SIMILAR SPECIES The commoner False Saffron Milkcap (p.100) has a smooth stem and grows under spruce.

This species is frequently confused with Saffron Milkcap (p.99) but is much commoner, especially in spruce plantations. The yellow-orange cap is zoned with darker rings, and old specimens or those exposed to frost show considerable greening. The shortly decurrent, pale-orange gills release a bitter orange milk that turns wine-red and finally dark green. The stem is only rarely pitted at its base.

SIZE Cap 5–12 cm, stem 3–7 cm x 10–15 mm.
HABITAT Always under spruce.
SEASON Late summer to autumn.
INEDIBLE Cooking reduces the bitterness. Not recommended.
SIMILAR SPECIES Saffron Milkcap (p.99) has orange pits at the stem base and a mild-tasting, orange milk. It grows with pines.

This species is an important wood rotter. The cap is mid to dark brown and smooth except for darker streaks, most prominent at the centre. The gills are free of the stem, crowded and initially white; later they take on a flesh-pink tinge as the pink spores mature. The solid, slender, white stem is streaked with dark-brown fibres and swollen at the base. It has a faint radish smell.

SIZE Cap 6–12 cm, stem 4–10 cm x 8–12 mm.
HABITAT On broad-leaved stumps and logs. Also on woodchip piles. Rare on coniferous wood.
SEASON All year but most frequent in autumn.
EDIBLE Not highly rated due to its sharp taste.
SIMILAR SPECIES *Volvariella gloiocephala* also has free, pink gills but a creamy-brown cap. Stem emerges from a volva. Grows in gardens, stubble and on sawdust.

Although not as common as Deer Shield (p.101) this beautiful fungus is frequent in the same habitat. The broadly convex, sepia-brown cap is overlain with branching veins of dark-brown, tiny, velvety scales; especially near the centre. The crowded, free gills start white but mature pink with a dark-brown edge. The pale-brown stem has cap-like scales. It smells faintly of garlic.

SIZE Cap 4–9 cm, stem 3–8 cm x 8–12 mm.
HABITAT On stumps and well-rotted wood of broad-leaved trees.
SEASON Late summer to autumn.
EDIBLE Soft-fleshed and not highly recommended.
SIMILAR SPECIES Deer Shield (p.101) lacks the vein-like, velvety scales on its cap. *P. chrysophaeus* has a smaller, smoother, ochre-yellow cap.

This common species typifies the genus with its pink gills and pink, angular spores. It was previously called *Nolanea sericea*. The convex cap expands flat with a central umbo. It smells of meal. The young cap is moist, dark brown with a grooved margin, later fading from the centre to creamy-beige with a silky surface. The sinuate gills have a ragged edge and mature grey-pink; a pink spore print can be seen at the apex of the stem.

SIZE Cap 2–5 cm, stem 3–5 cm x 2–4 mm.
HABITAT On lawns and short grass; often in troops.
SEASON Midsummer to autumn.
INEDIBLE Confusable with poisonous pink-spored species.
SIMILAR SPECIES The Miller (p.108) smells of meal and has deeply decurrent, pale-pink gills.

Star Pinkgill

ENTOLOMATACEAE FAMILY

Entoloma conferendum

Like the previous species, older caps become flat and fade to pale ochre but *E. conferendum* has a more fleshy, bell-shaped, russet-brown young cap, sticky when moist and markedly striated near its margin. It has crowded, adnexed, pale-pink gills. The slender stem is striated with grey fibres and broadens at the base. Formerly known as *Nolanea staurospora*.

SIZE Cap 3–5 cm, stem 4–8 cm x 3–6 mm.

HABITAT Pasture, lawns and grassy woods. Also on moorland.

SEASON Midsummer to autumn.

INEDIBLE Too easily confused with poisonous species.

SIMILAR SPECIES The larger *E. rhodopolium* is found in damp woods, often under willow. Pale-brown cap has a striate margin and dries to a silky dirty-white.

The young convex cap has a broad central umbo but matures funnel-shaped with a central depression. It is dry, creamy-white and slightly rough. The gills, quite spaced, are initially white but age pink. Stem slender, white and shiny. It has a pleasant mushroomy smell. Previously called *Leptonia sericella*.

SIZE Cap 2–4 cm, stem 2–5 cm x 2–3 mm.
HABITAT Wet grassland, often among moss.
SEASON Late summer to autumn.
INEDIBLE Beware confusion with highly poisonous fungi.
SIMILAR SPECIES The Miller (p.108) has a mealy smell as does the very poisonous Ivory Funnel (p.33) but this has crowded, white gills and a white spore print. Snowy Waxcap (p.66) has broad, distant gills.

There are a number of small, dark-blue species with pink spores that were previously placed in the *Leptonia* genus. The photograph shows the blue-black colour (the French describe it as crow-like) of young convex caps and the paler, flat, older caps, which have a roughly fibrous margin. The adnate, white gills mature pale pink. The slender stem has a white base.

SIZE Cap 1–3 cm, stem 2–6 cm x 2–3 mm.
HABITAT In unimproved short grassland.
SEASON Summer to autumn.
POISONOUS Some blue Pinkgills are poisonous, so avoid.
SIMILAR SPECIES *E. serrulatum* has grey-pink gills with a distinctive black edge and is more common in upland pasture.

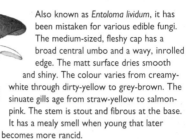

Also known as *Entoloma lividum*, it has been mistaken for various edible fungi. The medium-sized, fleshy cap has a broad central umbo and a wavy, inrolled edge. The matt surface dries smooth and shiny. The colour varies from creamy-white through dirty-yellow to grey-brown. The sinuate gills age from straw-yellow to salmon-pink. The stem is stout and fibrous at the base. It has a mealy smell when young that later becomes more rancid.

SIZE Cap 6–18 cm, stem 5–10 cm x 15–20 mm.
HABITAT Field edges, open woodland with beech or oak on rich soil.
SEASON Autumn, rarely also in spring.
POISONOUS Causes gastric upset and liver damage.
SIMILAR SPECIES St George's Mushroom (p.62) has a similar size, shape and smell but has white gills and spores.

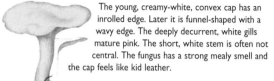

The young, creamy-white, convex cap has an inrolled edge. Later it is funnel-shaped with a wavy edge. The deeply decurrent, white gills mature pink. The short, white stem is often not central. The fungus has a strong mealy smell and the cap feels like kid leather.

SIZE Cap 4–10 cm, stem 3–4 cm x 6–12 mm.

HABITAT Among grass in open woodland.

SEASON Late summer to autumn.

EDIBLE Excellent; the firm flesh tastes of meal. Beware confusion with poisonous species (see below).

SIMILAR SPECIES The poisonous Ivory Funnel (p.33), though smaller, has a similar shape and habitat. The gills are only weakly decurrent and the spore print is white, not pink.

This once rare species became commoner (especially in S. England) following Dutch elm disease but is declining again. The broadly convex cap is wrinkled and gelatinous. It starts deep pink with an inrolled edge but matures flatter and apricot-coloured. The sinuate, crowded gills are paler than the cap and have cross-connecting veins. The pale-pink stem is often curved. The fungus smells of apricots.

SIZE Cap 5–10 cm, stem 3–6 cm x 8–12 mm.
HABITAT On stumps and fallen dead elm; also on beech, ash and sycamore.
SEASON Early autumn to winter.
INEDIBLE The flesh has a very bitter taste.
SIMILAR SPECIES Not easily confused with other species.

A thin-fleshed, fragile little species, also known as the Egg Yolk Fungus. The young cap is distinctly conical and the centre is shiny, slimy and egg-yolk yellow; the margin paler and grooved. Older caps are flat, pale ochre-brown with a translucent edge. The straw-coloured gills mature rusty-brown. The delicate, pale-yellow stem is more slender when growing in long grass.

SIZE Cap 1–3 cm, stem 5–10 cm x 2–4 mm.

HABITAT Often solitary; on dung, rotting hay or straw, compost and well-manured grassland.

SEASON Late summer to autumn.

INEDIBLE Insubstantial and with a slimy texture.

SIMILAR SPECIES Pleated Inkcap (p.143) has black spores.

Common in short grass where it is frequently confused with other small, brown-capped species. The orange to ochre-brown cap remains bell-shaped with a striate margin when moist but dries yellowy-cream. The crowded, brown gills ascend to the stem apex. The delicate, pale-ochre stem has a powdered surface.

SIZE Cap 1–3 cm, stem 4–8 cm x 2–4 mm.
HABITAT Among grass in lawns, pasture and open woodland.
SEASON Late spring to late autumn.
INEDIBLE Insubstantial.
SIMILAR SPECIES Some related *Conocybe* species are not easily distinguished. Magic Mushroom (p.120) has a pointed cap and almost black gills. Dung Roundhead (p.119) has a hemispherical cap and dark-brown gills.

The small- to medium-sized cap is broadly convex, with a pale-tan colour that soon fades to creamy-beige. Initially a cream-coloured veil covers the gills; later it shows as remnants at the cap margin and an insubstantial ring high on the stem. The crowded, cream-coloured gills mature dingy-brown. The stem is paler than the cap and has a bulbous base.

SIZE Cap 3–6 cm, stem 7–9 cm x 6–12 mm.
HABITAT In grass often in open woods and under hedges.
SEASON Spring to summer. Occasionally in autumn.
EDIBLE Must be well cooked; not recommended.
SIMILAR SPECIES Can be confused with Field Mushroom (p.132), which has a fleshier cap and free gills that start pink but age very dark brown.

The broadly convex, yellow-ochre cap is covered in concentric
rings of upturned, triangular, red-brown scales. The margin remains
inrolled. The crowded, straw-coloured, adnate gills mature rusty-
brown. The long, often curved stem narrows at its base. Below the
scruffy ring are cap-like scales; above it is paler and smooth. It has
a sharp, radish-like smell.

SIZE Cap 4–12 cm, stem 6–15 cm x 7–15 mm.
HABITAT Clustered at the base of living
trunks or standing, dead, broad-leaved trees,
especially on beech and ash, but also rowan and
many other species.
SEASON Summer to autumn.
INEDIBLE The bitter flesh is difficult to digest.
SIMILAR SPECIES Two yellow species – *P. flammans*
grows on conifers, *P. alnicola* on alder and birch.

Pholiota highlandensis

A small fungus frequently found on old bonfire sites hence its common name and the former Latin name, *P. carbonaria*. It has an orange-brown cap, shiny and slightly sticky with a paler, often wavy margin. The crowded, adnate gills are clay-brown with an olive tint. The stem is paler than the cap at the apex but darker near the base where it is covered in tiny red-brown scales. The ring zone soon disappears. It has no distinctive smell.

SIZE Cap 2–6 cm, stem 3–6 cm x 4–8 mm.
HABITAT In troops on charred wood and burnt ground.
SEASON Autumn to early winter.
INEDIBLE Insubstantial.
SIMILAR SPECIES The specific habitat of Bonfire Scalycap distinquishes it from related species.

Brown and shiny when moist, the centre of the cap
readily dries to pale tan – hence '*mutabilis*'. The
crowded, adnexed gills darken from cream to russet-
brown. The slender, often curved stem is pale tan
and smooth above the ragged ring (which often
disappears) but dark brown from the small scales
nearer its base.

SIZE Cap 3–8 cm, stem 3–8 cm x 4–8 mm
HABITAT In tufts on broad-leaved stumps and logs.
SEASON Spring to winter.
EDIBLE Good to eat but see below.
SIMILAR SPECIES The poisonous *Galerina marginata* grows as tufts
on both coniferous and broad-leaved wood. The brown gills are
white-edged and the stem lacks brown scales. See also Velvet Shank
(p.54) and Sulphur Tuft (p.116).

Sulphur Tuft

STROPHARIACEAE FAMILY

Hypholoma fasiculare

The young caps are bell-shaped, smooth and rich sulphur-yellow, with gills covered by a pale, cobweb-like veil. They are later convex with a tan centre and pale-yellow margin, often bearing veil remnants, now darkened by the spores. The gills are crowded, initially yellow but later olive-green to black from the spores. The slender stem curves at its base. There is a purple-brown ring zone.

SIZE Cap 2–6 cm, stem 5–12 cm x 5–10 mm.
HABITAT In tufts on stumps and dead wood of broad-leaved trees; also on conifers.
SEASON Throughout the year.
POISONOUS Very bitter with a taste like quinine.
SIMILAR SPECIES Brick Tuft (p.117). Velvet Shank (p.54).

Similar to the previous species but with fewer in a
tuft. The fleshy caps are brick-red near the centre
and pale tan at the margin, which typically bears
white veil remnants. The creamy-yellow, adnate gills
mature grey-brown. The stem is yellow above the dark-
brown ring zone, increasingly red-brown below.

SIZE Cap 4–8 cm, stem 6–10 cm x 8–12 mm.
HABITAT Usually on oak stumps. Also on dead roots.
SEASON Autumn.
INEDIBLE Less bitter than Sulphur Tuft but not edible.
SIMILAR SPECIES The much less common *H. capnoides* has a
slightly sticky, tan-coloured cap and grey gills. It grows on conifer
stumps. Mild-tasting and edible but do not mistake for Sulphur
Tuft (p.116).

Blue Roundhead

**STROPHARIACEAE
FAMILY**

Stropharia caerulea

Fresh specimens have slimy, shiny caps; young ones are dark, blue-green and bell-shaped, older ones more convex and grass-green. The cap margin is peppered with small, white scales. Old caps lack slime and scales. The crowded, sinuate gills start pale grey but age purple-brown. The stem is white above the transient ring (coloured by the purple-black spores); it is pale blue-green with white scales below.

SIZE Cap 2–6 cm, stem 4–8 cm x 5–10 mm.
HABITAT In woods, gardens and parkland.
SEASON Midsummer to autumn.
POISONOUS The colour is off-putting!
SIMILAR SPECIES *S. aeruginosa*, previously known as Verdigris Toadstool, has a bluer cap with persistent white scales, white-edged gills and a more persistent ring. The two species were not previously distinguished.

A very common small, brown fungus with an unusual shape likened to half a marble on a match stick. The hemispherical, ochre cap rarely flattens and is slimy when moist, sticky when dry. The adnate, crowded gills do not ascend before joining the stem. The young, pale-grey gills age dark brown. The pale-yellow, slender stem is sticky below a transient ring.

SIZE Cap 1–3 cm, stem 4–10 cm x 2–3 mm.
HABITAT In and by dung in pasture and on manured soil.
SEASON Late spring to late autumn.
INEDIBLE Insubstantial and slimy-textured.

SIMILAR SPECIES
Dung-loving species of *Panaeolina* and *Panaeolus* (pp.146 & 149) have bell-shaped caps and mottled-brown gills. Magic Mushroom (p.120) has a pointed cap, ascending gills and a wavy stem.

Magic Mushroom

STROPHARIACEAE FAMILY

Psilocybe semilanceata

Previously known as Liberty Cap, the new name came in during the 1960s along with its notoriety as a hallucinogen. The bell-shaped cap usually narrows to a point. Slimy and date-brown when moist, it dries pale straw, often with a furrowed margin. The crowded gills ascend to the stem apex. Initially grey, they mature almost black with a white edge. The slender, wavy stem blues at the base.

SIZE Cap 0.5–1.5 cm, stem 2–5 cm x 2–3 mm.
HABITAT In grass (lawns, playing fields, pastures).
SEASON Summer to autumn.
POISONOUS Hallucinogenic. Collecting is illegal.
SIMILAR SPECIES *P. coprophila* and *P. merdaria* grow on dung. *P. cyanescens* with date-brown, flat caps and stems that discolour blue is increasing on woodchip.

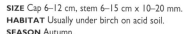

There are over 200 species of *Cortinarius*. One of the more frequent, *C. armillatus* has a rust-coloured, fleshy cap with slightly darker fibres near the centre and red-brown cobweb veil remnants at the margin. It has adnate, rusty-brown gills. The chunky, pale-tan stem is encircled by one or more orange-red bands and is swollen at its base.

SIZE Cap 6–12 cm, stem 6–15 cm x 10–20 mm.
HABITAT Usually under birch on acid soil.
SEASON Autumn.
INEDIBLE Some species (see below) are very poisonous.
SIMILAR SPECIES The deadly poisonous *C. rubellus* has a smaller cap and yellow veil remnants on a tawny stem. With conifers.

Cortinarius purpurascens

The slimy/shiny, wavy-edged cap is a mix of grey-brown and violet. There is a cobweb-like veil (cortina) with purple hue. The purple gills brown with age as the spores develop. The broad, cap-coloured stem has a swollen base and bruises violet. The flesh is purple with a faint fruity smell.

SIZE Cap 5–12 cm, stem 6–12 cm x 15–25 mm.
HABITAT Under broad-leaved and coniferous trees.
SEASON Autumn.
INEDIBLE Reported to produce digestive upset, so avoid.
SIMILAR SPECIES *C. violaceus* has a dark violet cap, gills and stem. *C. largus* has pale-lilac tints on the cap, gills and stem. *C. mucifluoides* has a sticky, brown cap, pale-edged brown gills and a violet stem base.

A small Webcap with a distinctive deep carmine-red cap, gills, flesh and stem. The cap is covered with minute, silky fibres. The red gills darken as the rusty-brown spores mature. The stem base is covered in a pale down.

SIZE Cap 2–5 cm, stem 3–6 cm x 3–8 mm.
HABITAT Found on acid soil under coniferous, broad-leaved and mixed woodland.
SEASON Autumn.
POISONOUS Confusable with the very poisonous *C. rubellus*.
SIMILAR SPECIES *C. semisanguineus* has red gills but a yellow-brown cap and stem. *C. cinnabarinus* (under beech) has all parts orange-red.

One of the largest woodland Fibrecaps with a fleshy, silky, conical cap. Typically cream- to straw-coloured, it ages brick-red on the radiating fibres and when bruised. The crowded, adnexed gills start pale pink but age olive-yellow and bruise brick-red, as does the stout, white stem. The smell is fruity, later becoming foetid and unpleasant.

SIZE Cap 3–8 cm, stem 3–10 cm x 10–15 mm.

HABITAT In grass at woodland edges; mostly on chalk, with beech and hazel.

SEASON June to late summer.

POISONOUS Causes death by heart failure or asphyxiation.

SIMILAR SPECIES The edible St George's Mushroom (p.62) has white gills, does not stain red and smells of meal.

Its conical cap often splits at the margin when expanded but retains a raised, pale-brown central area. The rest of the cap is straw-yellow and covered with grey-brown, radiating fibres. The gills are crowded and olive-brown. The slim, pale stem is not swollen at its base. Formerly known as *I. fastigiata*.

SIZE Cap 3–7 cm, stem 5–8 cm x 5–10 mm.
HABITAT Broad-leaved woods, especially with beech and oak.
SEASON Midsummer to autumn.
POISONOUS Dangerous due to its muscarine content.
SIMILAR SPECIES *I. maculata* has darker-brown fibrils and white down at the cap centre. *I. asterospora* also has brown fibrils but a fawn-coloured stem with a very swollen base.

White Fibrecap

CORTINARIACEAE FAMILY

Inocybe geophylla

This little fungus occurs in both a white form and with a lilac cap and stem in var. *lilacina* (Lilac Fibrecap). The conical cap flattens but keeps a central umbo. The adnexed, crowded gills mature from cream to dirty-brown. The thin stem is covered with silky fibres.

SIZE Cap 1–4 cm, stem 2–5 cm x 3–4 mm.
HABITAT Gregarious, often by paths in woods.
SEASON Summer to autumn.
POISONOUS Dangerous, as the lilac form is easily confused with edibles.
SIMILAR SPECIES Both forms look like Bonnets (pp. 42–49), which have white spores. Lilac Fibrecap is confused with Amethyst Deceiver (p.26), but this has widely spaced, purple gills and white spores. *I. griseolilacina* is paler lilac and has small, brown scales at the cap centre.

A common brown fungus that beginners find difficult to identify. The convex, pale-tan, smooth cap is sticky when moist, with an inrolled margin. The adnate, grey-brown gills have a pale margin that exudes drops of water (not easily seen). The apex of the tan stem is covered with mealy, white scales that rub off with handling. Sharp smell of radish or freshly cut, raw potato.

SIZE Cap 4–10 cm, stem 4–7 cm x 5–10 mm.
HABITAT Under broad-leaved trees, often with birch.
SEASON Early autumn to early winter.
POISONOUS Very bitter, causing gastric upset.
SIMILAR SPECIES The smaller *H. anthracophilum* is darker, has a pliable stem and grows on burnt ground. *H. sinapizans* has sinuate gills and is commonest under beech.

Found on acidic or sandy soils, it grows under conifers and broad-leaved trees. The broadly convex cap is slimy and a rich chestnut-brown at the centre, pale creamy-brown at the margin. The crowded, pinky-brown gills are protected by a cobweb-like veil when young. The white stem sometimes has a faint brown ring zone (veil remnants) about halfway up and widens to a brown base. It has a faint smell of radish.

SIZE Cap 2–5 cm, stem 4–7 cm x 5–12 mm.
HABITAT Under pines and other trees, especially birch.
SEASON Late summer to autumn.
INEDIBLE Avoid as related species are poisonous.
SIMILAR SPECIES *H. pusillum* has a similar cap colour but clay-brown gills. Under willows on moist soil.

This attractive fungus is rusty- or tawny-brown on its cap, gills and stem. The medium-sized, bell-shaped cap soon flattens but often has a wavy margin. It is thin-fleshed and with a dry, silky feel. The crowded, pale-yellow, adnate to weakly decurrent gills darken with age and discolour with rust-coloured spots. The golden stem is darker below its middle and has a white, woolly base. Young stems bear a fibrillose ring.

SIZE Cap 4–8 cm, stem 4–7 cm x 5–8 mm.
HABITAT On dead conifer wood and chippings, rare on birch and oak.
SEASON Late summer to autumn.
INEDIBLE Tough and with bitter-tasting flesh.
SIMILAR SPECIES Spectacular Rustgill (p.130) is much larger. In tufts on dead wood of broad-leaved trees.

Spectacular Rustgill

CORTINARIACEAE FAMILY

Gymnopilus junonius

Known as the 'Laughing Mushroom' in Japan, its large, dry, fleshy, convex cap retains a broad umbo after expanding. A vivid golden-orange, it is covered by tiny, flattened, similar-coloured, fibrous scales. The adnate, yellow gills age rusty-orange. The thick stem is often broader in the lower region before narrowing to a root-like base. Young specimens have a shaggy ring covered with rusty spores.

SIZE Cap 6–15 cm, stem 6–18 cm x 15–30 mm.
HABITAT In clusters from the base of broad-leaved trees. Also on stumps, rotting logs and from buried wood.
SEASON Summer to early winter.
INEDIBLE Bitter. May contain psilocybin.
SIMILAR SPECIES *Pholiota alnicola* is smooth and yellow.

A tiny fungus with a
bell-shaped, shiny,
russet-brown cap and
a ribbed margin. The
adnate gills are rust-
coloured with a white
edge. The slim, tan
stem is browner near
the base and covered
with a bloom near the
apex.

SIZE Cap 1–2 cm, stem 3–6 cm x 1–2 mm.
HABITAT Among moss in woods, heaths
and grassland.
SEASON Spring to autumn.
INEDIBLE Too small to be worth eating.
SIMILAR SPECIES Also growing in moss,
G. hypnorum has a honey-brown cap and a
mealy smell. *G. paludosa* grows with bog
moss. Orange Mosscap (p.50) has
decurrent gills and white spores.

This is the best known of about 40 species of *Agaricus*. The young (button) white cap is firm, smooth and domed. It expands flat and the centre may bear small, pale-brown scales. The initially inrolled margin bears untidy veil remnants. The young gills are protected by a white veil; they are crowded and free. They change from deep pink through brown to black. There is a transient ring on the stocky, white stem. It has a pleasant smell.

SIZE Cap 3–10 cm, stem 3–7 cm x 10–15 mm.
HABITAT Among short grass in pasture, lawns, playing fields and cemeteries.
SEASON Early summer to late autumn; following rain.
EDIBLE Excellent. Can be eaten raw but see below.
SIMILAR SPECIES Yellow Stainer (p.135) is poisonous to some; it has an unpleasant smell.

The brown form of our shop-bought mushroom is occasionally found in the wild. The mature caps are typically darker than Field Mushroom due to a covering of brown, fibre-like scales. The crowded, free gills are pink in young specimens; very dark brown in old flat caps. The stem bears a permanent, large, white, shaggy ring. Unlike Field Mushroom, the cut flesh reddens slightly.

SIZE Cap 3–10 cm, stem 3–6 cm x 10–15 mm.

HABITAT Grassland, in rich soil, dung heaps and mushroom compost.

SEASON Summer to autumn.

EDIBLE Can be eaten raw. Older ones have more flavour.

SIMILAR SPECIES Specimens with dark-brown caps can be confused with some woodland mushrooms (p.136).

A large, fleshy species smelling of aniseed or bitter almonds. The deeply domed, young, white cap matures flat. Mostly smooth but may break up into scales at the margin. Older caps have an ochre tinge and flush dull yellow-ochre when bruised. The free, grey gills mature dark-brown. The white stem also bruises yellow-ochre. The swollen base does not yellow when cut. It has a large, two-layered ring, with an underside like a cogwheel.

SIZE Cap 5–20 cm, stem 5–15 cm x 15–20 mm.
HABITAT Permanent pastures and road verges; often in rings. Horses not necessary!
SEASON Early summer to late autumn.
EDIBLE Excellent flavour and texture but see below.
SIMILAR SPECIES See the poisonous Yellow Stainer (p.135).

This species causes sickness and diarrhoea in a substantial minority. The button stage is unusual in that it is flat-topped. The white cap is minutely scaly at the centre and on bruising rapidly turns bright yellow, especially near the margin. The young, white gills turn grey-pink and finally dark brown. The white stem bears a large, down-turned ring and a swollen base, the cut flesh of which turns chrome-yellow. It has an unpleasant smell, like ink or stale urine.

SIZE Cap 5–10 cm, stem 6–10 cm x 10–18 mm.
HABITAT In grassland, gardens, hedgerows and woods.
SEASON Summer to autumn.
POISONOUS Many people are unaffected but best avoided.
SIMILAR SPECIES The cap of the edible *A. silvicola* (Wood Mushroom) bruises bright yellow but the cut stem does not.

The hazel-brown cap surface breaks into small, fibrous scales. The pale-pink, free gills age darker and bruise red on handling. The tall, hollow, white stem is minutely scaly below the large, floppy, brown ring and bruises dark red. The cut flesh in the stem and cap also reddens. It has a faint mushroomy smell.

SIZE Cap 8–12 cm, stem 8–10 cm x 15–20 mm.

HABITAT On soil in coniferous and mixed woodlands.

SEASON Autumn.

EDIBLE Good to eat despite the 'bleeding flesh'.

SIMILAR SPECIES The stem and large, scaly cap of The Prince (*A. augustus*) stain dull yellow on bruising, as does the cut flesh, which smells of aniseed. Edible.

Initially most of the stem is hidden beneath the finger-shaped, smooth, white cap, which becomes rugby-ball shaped with a smooth, dirty-brown apex; the rest breaks up into white or pale-brown, shaggy scales. The cap base expands and dissolves into an inky fluid, resulting in a small, flat cap on a long stem. The crowded, free gills hang down and change from white through pink to black. The smooth, white, hollow stem has a transient ring.

SIZE Cap 5–15 cm, stem 8–30 cm x 10–15 mm.

HABITAT Grass, woodland vegetation and urban sites.

SEASON Spring to early winter.

EDIBLE Must be eaten young. Good salty flavour.

SIMILAR SPECIES See Common Inkcap (p.138) and Magpie Inkcap (p.139), both of which are now put in a different family.

The grey to fawn cap is initially egg-shaped, later bell-shaped. The smooth surface breaks into a few tiny scales at the apex; the margin is often wavy and split. The ascending gills mature from white to grey and finally black when they dissolve into an inky fluid. It has a smooth, hollow, white stem with an ill-defined ring zone.

SIZE Cap 4–8 cm, stem 5–15 cm x 10–15 mm.
HABITAT Gregarious from tree stumps or in grass, gardens, pavements – wherever buried wood is present.
SEASON Spring to early winter.
POISONOUS It reacts with alcohol in the bloodstream, causing nausea and hot flushes.
SIMILAR SPECIES The woodland *C. acuminata* is smaller and grows on wet, rotten wood.

The young, finger-shaped, white cap is similar to that of the Shaggy Inkcap (p.137), but as the stem lengthens the cap becomes more bell-shaped and the white breaks into patches on a dark-brown background. The pale-pink, ascending gills turn black and dissolve into an ink-like fluid. The white stem has a slightly frosted surface and lacks a ring. It smells of tar.

SIZE Cap 6–10 cm, stem 10–20 cm x 15–20 mm.

HABITAT Under broad-leaved trees, mostly with beech.

SEASON Autumn.

INEDIBLE Unpleasant smell. Possibly poisonous.

SIMILAR SPECIES The much smaller *C. cinerea* grows on steaming compost, dung and manure. White scales mostly confined to the apex of the grey-black, conical cap.

Beginners often confuse this with Glistening Inkcap (p.141) but the shaggy, rust-coloured vegetative strands at the stem base help to separate them. The bell-shaped, tan-coloured cap has a rusty-brown apex dusted with white granular scales and a grooved margin. The crowded, white gills age dark grey with a purple tint before finally dissolving. The smooth, white stem has a swollen base.

SIZE Cap 2–5 cm, stem 4–8 cm x 4–5 mm.
HABITAT On dead wood and stumps of broad-leaved trees. Rare on conifer wood. Not clustered.

SEASON Early summer to early autumn.
INEDIBLE Not worth eating.
SIMILAR SPECIES The much less common *C. xanthothrix* also grows from a rust-coloured mat but has pale-brown cap scales. Glistening Inkcap (p.141) lacks the rust mat.

More easily identified from young specimens when the ochre-brown, bell-shaped caps are dusted with similar-coloured, glistening, mica-like grains. The older caps lose these and the grooved margin often splits and turns up. The crowded, pale gills age brown, then black, before finally dissolving into a black fluid. The white stem browns at its base.

SIZE Cap 2–4 cm, stem 5–8 cm x 2–4 mm.
HABITAT In dense clusters on broad-leaved stumps and logs. Also from dead roots.
SEASON Throughout the year.
EDIBLE Hardly worthwhile; poor flavour and texture.
SIMILAR SPECIES Frequently confused with Firerug Inkcap (p.140), which has white grains and grows from a rust-coloured mat.

This tiny fungus would probably pass unnoticed but for the fact that it grows in very large groups; often several hundred together. The young, oval-shaped, pale-beige caps mature bell-shaped, markedly grooved and greyer, though the apex remains brown. The pale-grey gills darken with age but show little of the autodigesting (dissolving to an inky fluid) of other Inkcaps. The spindly, fragile, grey-white stem has a downy base.

SIZE Cap 0.5–1.5 cm, stem 2–4 cm x 1–2 mm.

HABITAT Large clusters on and near rotting wood.

SEASON Spring to early winter.

EDIBLE Too insubstantial to be worthwhile.

SIMILAR SPECIES The habit of growing in such large groups distinguishes it from other related species.

A very delicate fungus common in short grass and unusual for an Inkcap in having a cap that finally flattens and shrivels rather than dissolving to a black ink. Initially pale tan, the paper-thin, ribbed, translucent cap turns grey apart from a brown central disc. The thin, spaced, grey-black gills radiate from a collar round the easily broken, tall, slender stem. Formerly called Fairy Parasol.

SIZE Cap 1–2 cm, stem 4–6 cm x 2–3 mm.
HABITAT In short grass.
SEASON Spring to early winter.
EDIBLE Far too insubstantial to be worth collecting.
SIMILAR SPECIES A number of related species, e.g.
P. auricoma, have browner caps, and are found
beneath trees and on woodchip.

Only old caps show the dark gill and spore colour, so Brittlestems are frequently confused with white- and pink-spored species. This one has a thin-fleshed, ochre-yellow cap that soon flattens and dries pale cream, especially near the margin, which frequently splits and bears dark veil remnants. The gills are crowded, adnexed and initially white then lilac-grey before turning dark brown. The cap does not dissolve. The stem is thin, white and brittle.

SIZE Cap 3–6 cm, stem 5–8 cm x 3–5 mm.
HABITAT On woodland soil and stumps. Also in grass.
SEASON Early summer to autumn.
EDIBLE Said to be edible if cooked but not worthwhile.
SIMILAR SPECIES There are many Brittlestems; most grow in small groups on soil or among grass.

A densely tufted species, common on stumps. The neatly convex young caps are a beautiful, shiny date-brown with small, white veil fragments at the margins. As the cap ages it flattens and dries pale tan from the centre, giving a two-toned appearance. The young, pale-brown, crowded gills blacken as the spores mature. The fragile, smooth, white stem darkens near its base.

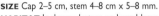

SIZE Cap 2–5 cm, stem 4–8 cm x 5–8 mm.
HABITAT In dense clusters on broad-leaved tree stumps, dead roots and other debris.
SEASON Early summer to late autumn.
EDIBLE Not recommended due to its bitter taste.
SIMILAR SPECIES Sheathed Woodtuft (p.115) is also tufted on stumps but has a ring and scaly, brown stem base.

Like the previous species, this has a two-toned, brown, convex cap. As the picture shows, some may be all date-brown and others much paler. The ascending, pale-brown gills later become mottled with black patches from the ripe spores. The stem is slender, smooth and brown. Also known as Hay Cap.

SIZE Cap 1–2 cm, stem 4–6 cm x 2–3 mm.
HABITAT Among short and mown grass.
SEASON Midsummer to autumn.
POISONOUS May produce hallucinations.
SIMILAR SPECIES *Panaeolus acuminatus* (*rickenii*) has a bell-shaped, red-brown cap and a white bloom on its dark-brown stem. Brown Conecap (p.111) has rusty-brown gills. Magic Mushroom (p.120) has a pointed cap and unmottled, dark-brown gills.

The broadly convex, yellow-brown cap maintains a central umbo. When young it is covered with darker fibres and has a shaggy margin due to veil fragments that blacken as the spores develop. The crowded, adnate gills are mottled brown and black with a white edge. In moist weather watery droplets are exuded near the junction of gill and stem. The stem has brown fibres and a ring zone blackened by the spores. Listed in some books as *L. velutina*.

SIZE Cap 5–10 cm, stem 6–10 cm x 6–10 mm.
HABITAT Often on disturbed ground in lawns and open woodland.
SEASON Early summer to late autumn.
EDIBLE Firm-fleshed if a little bitter.
SIMILAR SPECIES Pale Brittlestem (p.144) is more thin-fleshed and less substantial.

Found on horse or cow dung, this is much larger than Brown Mottlegill (p.146) and Petticoat Mottlegill (p.149). The cap remains bell-shaped with a wrinkled, uneven surface. It is creamy-ochre; sticky when moist, and shiny when dry – like an egg-shell. The ascending brown and

black, mottled gills have a paler edge. The creamy-white stem bears a ring, later blackened by the spores.

SIZE Cap 2–6 cm, stem 5–15 cm x 4–8 mm.
HABITAT On horse and cow dung or in gardens on manure.
SEASON Summer to early winter.
INEDIBLE Its dung habitat makes it unsuitable for eating.
SIMILAR SPECIES Other *Panaeolus* species are smaller, darker and lack a ring.

A common, small, grassland species usually growing on dung, it gets its name from the cap margin, which is fringed with triangular, white veil fragments. The deeply bell-shaped cap varies from grey to almost black when moist but dries grey-brown. The adnate, brown gills are mottled with black patches (its alternative name is Grey Mottlegill). The grey-brown stem is long, slender and covered with a white bloom in the upper region.

SIZE Cap 2–4 cm, stem 6–12 cm x 2–3 mm.
HABITAT In grazed grassland; on or near dung.
SEASON Early summer to autumn.
POISONOUS May produce hallucinations.
SIMILAR SPECIES A variety with a browner cap and fewer veil remnants is found on horse dung.

Cep

BOLEACEAE FAMILY

Boletus edulis

Cep or Penny Bun has densely packed tubes in place of gills. The young, deeply convex caps are often wrinkled and narrower than the broad stem but expand to a large, fleshy, shallow dome-shape. The cap is mid-brown with paler patches and sticky when moist. The pores (tube ends) are small and white, ageing straw to olive-yellow. The very swollen pale-brown stem is overlain by a raised, white honeycomb network most obvious at the stem apex.

SIZE Cap 8–30 cm, stem 8–25 cm x 4–10 cm.
HABITAT Woodlands; with oak, beech, birch and pine. In grassland with rockrose.
SEASON Early summer to autumn.
EDIBLE Young ones can be pickled. Old ones dry well. Excellent texture and flavour.
SIMILAR SPECIES See Bay Bolete (p.151) and Bitter Bolete (p.157).

Formerly known as *Xerocomus badius*. The cap is shiny, chestnut or bay-horse coloured; it is sticky and darker when wet. Cylindrical stem, streaked with cap colour. The pores are large, angular and pale yellow, rapidly turning blue-green on bruising. The pale-yellow flesh blues faintly when cut.

SIZE Cap 7–15 cm, stem 5–12 cm x 20–25 mm.
HABITAT In coniferous (especially pine) woodland on acid soil. Carries on fruiting after felling of conifers.
SEASON July to November.
EDIBLE Excellent and firm-fleshed when young. Pleasant mushroomy taste. Rarely maggot-infested. Dries well.
SIMILAR SPECIES Red Cracking Bolete and Suede Bolete (pp.152 & 153). The paler Cep (p.150) has a raised network on its broader stem.

Red Cracking Bolete

Boletus (Xerocomus) chrysenteron

Frequently confused with other Boletes. The shallowly convex, yellow-brown, dry cap later cracks to reveal a pale layer just below the surface. The large, angular, yellow pores age olive and bruise blue-green. The cylindrical stem is pale yellow at its apex but flushed red towards the base.

SIZE Cap 5–10 cm, stem 4–8 cm x 10–15 mm.
HABITAT Typically under beech, larch and even cedar, but not with oak.
SEASON Midsummer to late autumn.
EDIBLE Not recommended due to its soggy texture.
SIMILAR SPECIES Suede Bolete (p.153) has no red on the stem or beneath the cracks on the cap.
B. cisalpinus cracks to reveal red flesh and is probably more common.

Sometimes placed in the genus *Xerocomus*, it has a pale olive-yellow to light-brown, dry cap with a velvety feel. At maturity the surface cracks to reveal the pale-yellow flesh. The golden-yellow, angular pores are larger close to the stem and age olive-yellow. It blues faintly when bruised. The creamy-yellow stem often bends and narrows near its base.

SIZE Cap 3–10 cm, stem 4–10 cm x 10–20 mm.
HABITAT Under broad-leaved and coniferous trees.
SEASON Summer to late autumn.
EDIBLE Not recommended due to its poor flavour and soggy texture.
SIMILAR SPECIES A very variable species. Darker forms look like Bay Bolete (p.151) while some forms look like Red Cracking Bolete (p.152).

Large and solid. The yellow flesh in the cap and stem rapidly turns dark blue on cutting. The fleshy, broadly convex cap is usually dark olive-brown with a velvet surface when young; later smooth and glossy. The small, round, yellow pores mature deep orange-red and bruise dark blue. The yellow, club-shaped stem bruises blue and is covered with tiny, red-brown dots in the lower region.

SIZE Cap 8–20 cm, stem 6–12 cm x 20–40 mm.

HABITAT Under broad-leaved trees, especially oak on acidic soils.

SEASON Early summer to autumn.

POISONOUS Causes stomach upset, especially when raw.

SIMILAR SPECIES Lurid Bolete and Devil's Bolete (see p.155).

The yellow-brown, fleshy cap bears tubes with orange-red pores that, like the cap, stem and cut flesh, bruise blue-green. The broad stem is yellowish at the top but most of the rest is covered by a purple-red, longitudinally elongated net.

SIZE Cap 8–14 cm, stem 5–12 cm x 15–40 mm.
HABITAT Under beech, oak or lime on chalky soils. Also in grassland with rockrose.
SEASON Midsummer to autumn.
POISONOUS Causes digestive upset and may produce unpleasant symptoms with alcohol.
SIMILAR SPECIES Devil's Bolete (*B. satanas*) has a large, creamy-brown, wavy-margined cap. Small, yellow-red pores bruise blue-green, cut flesh smells unpleasant and slowly blues, stem has a very swollen base and a red net. Causes severe sickness but is rarely fatal.

Previously known as *Boletus piperatus*, it is smaller than most common Boletes. The orange-brown, smooth cap is slightly sticky when moist but frequently cracks when dry, and has a wavy margin. The cap flesh is yellow. The small, rusty-brown pores are larger and more angular close to the stem, which is often off-centre to the cap. The stem is red-brown, narrowing markedly to a bright-yellow base.

SIZE Cap 3–6 cm, stem 3–8 cm x 8–15 mm.
HABITAT Common under birch or pine on sandy soil. Also with beech and oak. Often with Fly Agaric (p.13).
SEASON Late summer to late autumn.
EDIBLE Used to add flavour but is very peppery.
SIMILAR SPECIES None with such a hot taste.

An occasional species that when young can be mistaken for Cep (p.150). The domed, mid-brown cap has a wavy edge that often overlaps the marginal tubes. The tiny, white pores turn flesh-coloured as the pink spores mature. The club-shaped, pale-ochre stem is covered with a brown, raised honeycomb network. The white cap flesh is odourless but tastes very bitter.

SIZE Cap 5–14 cm, stem 6–14 cm x 20–40 mm.
HABITAT Under both conifers and broad-leaved species (especially sweet chestnut, beech and oak), often on acid soils.
SEASON Summer to autumn.
INEDIBLE Extremely bitter taste.

SIMILAR SPECIES
Cep (p.150) is a similar colour but the pores age olive-yellow, the stem bears a white network and the spores are brown.

Species of *Leccinum* differ from *Boletus* in having tiny scales on a longer stem. When young, *L. versipelle* has a rounded, firm, brick-red cap; this matures to a large, convex, orange-brown, dry cap, often with a shaggy edge. The pores are small, round and dirty white; they age pale brown. The long stem tapers from a swollen base; white, covered by small, brown or black scales. The firm, pale-pink flesh turns blue-grey when cut and black on cooking.

SIZE Cap 12–25 cm, stem 12–20 cm x 30–40 mm.
HABITAT Under birch in open woods, scrub and heathland.
SEASON Early summer to autumn, often after rain.
EDIBLE Caps make good eating; the stems need peeling.
SIMILAR SPECIES Less common species with red-brown stem scales grow with oak, aspen and poplar.

Commoner than the preceding species and very variable, with a dull, grey-brown, smaller, spongy-textured cap and no overhanging margin. The tubes round the stem are much shorter than elsewhere. The tiny, grey pores bruise pale brown. The cylindrical, white stem is peppered with tiny, brown-black scales. The soft, white flesh does not usually change colour when cut but may turn pink.

SIZE Cap 5–10 cm, stem 8–15 cm x 20–30 mm.
HABITAT Under birch; locally abundant.
SEASON Early summer to autumn.
EDIBLE Soggy. Only young caps are worth eating.
SIMILAR SPECIES Easily confused with Orange Birch Bolete (p.158); this is larger, firmer and has flesh that blues on cutting.

Parasitic Bolete

Pseudoboletus (Boletus) parasiticus

This small, occasional Bolete is instantly recognisable as it is always found with Common Earthball (p.219). Mutualistic (each partner benefits) rather then parasitic. The pale, olive-brown, dry cap is initially velvety but cracks on maturity. The margin remains inrolled until old. The large, angular, golden-yellow pores age red-brown. The yellow-brown stem often narrows at its base and curves from the underside of the earthball.

SIZE Cap 2–5 cm, stem 3–6 cm x 8–12 mm.
HABITAT Singly or in small tufts on Common Earthball.
SEASON Autumn.
EDIBLE Not recommended as it is quite rare.
SIMILAR SPECIES No other Boletes are found attached to Earthballs.

Species of *Suillus* are distinguished from those of *Boletus* or *Leccinum* by their slimy caps and larger pore size. Larch Bolete (was *Boletus elegans*) has a slimy, golden-yellow cap that dries glossy. The pores are large, angular and initially covered by a pale-yellow veil that forms a ring on the stem. This drops off, leaving a paler area above which the yellow stem is scurfy.

SIZE Cap 4–12 cm, stem 5–10 cm x 12–18 mm.
HABITAT Under or close to larch, often in rings.
SEASON Summer to late autumn.
EDIBLE Remove slimy cap skin. Best in soups.
SIMILAR SPECIES *S. viscidus* has a wrinkled, flecked cap; *S. tridentinus* has compound, orange pores. Both grow with larch. Slippery Jack (p.162) is brown and grows under pine.

The only common slimy-capped Bolete with a persistent ring. The chestnut-brown cap finally dries smooth and shiny. The yellow pores are initially covered with a white veil; they brown with age and on bruising. The stem is pale yellow and scurfy above the floppy ring; creamy-brown below. The flesh is pale yellow and soft.

SIZE Cap 6–12 cm, stem 5–10 cm x 15–20 mm.
HABITAT Under pine trees on well-drained soil.

SEASON Late summer to autumn.
EDIBLE Remove slimy skin. Lacks flavour.
SIMILAR SPECIES Related species growing under pine include Bovine Bolete (p.163) and *S. granulatus*: both lack a ring and the latter exudes milky droplets from its pores and granular stem.

As both the common and Latin names suggest, this has a cow-like colour (e.g. Jersey) to its thin, slimy cap, which dries shiny with a paler margin. The large, angular, olive-yellow pores are frequently subdivided and are elongated near the stem, where the tubes are slightly decurrent. The smooth, cap-coloured, cylindrical stem lacks a ring and often bends at the base.

SIZE Cap 4–12 cm, stem 4–10 cm x 10–15 mm.
HABITAT In grass, moss and heather under Scots pine.
SEASON Late summer to autumn.
EDIBLE Poor flavour and rubbery texture.
SIMILAR SPECIES The larger, yellower Larch Bolete (p.161) grows with larch. Peppery Bolete (p.156) grows with pine but has a dry, matt cap and a peppery taste.

The very common Brown Rollrim has a convex young cap that finally becomes flat and even funnel-shaped but retains a shaggy, inrolled margin. The soft gills are easily removed from the cap, which is olive to rust-brown and slimy at the centre when moist. It bruises darker, as do the very crowded, decurrent, forking, brown gills and the pale-brown stem, which narrows from the apex.

SIZE Cap 7–15 cm, stem 4–8 cm x 10–20 mm.
HABITAT Under broad-leaved trees in woods and heaths; often with birch. Rarer with conifers and rockrose in grasslands.

SEASON Midsummer to late autumn.
POISONOUS Causes sickness and more serious illness.
SIMILAR SPECIES See Velvet Rollrim (p.165).

A wood rotter that grows on old conifer stumps. The large, chunky, irregular cap has a semicircular or shell-like outline. It is flat or centrally depressed, with an inrolled, smooth margin. The dingy-brown surface is dry and velvety when young, smoother with age. The decurrent, crowded, creamy-yellow gills fork near the short, broad, velvety, laterally attached, brown-black stem. Previously called *Paxillus atrotomentosus*.

SIZE Cap 8–25 cm,
stem 4–8 cm x 20–50 mm.
HABITAT Clustered on or near conifer stumps, mostly on pine.
SEASON Midsummer to autumn. More common in Scotland.
POISONOUS Bitter and similar to Brown Rollrim.
SIMILAR SPECIES Brown Rollrim (see p.164).

Frequently mistaken for Chanterelle (p.167) despite growing in different habitats. The dry, rather downy, funnel-shaped cap has an inrolled margin and depressed centre. Thin-fleshed, the whole fruitbody is orange-yellow but dries darker. It also occurs as a paler variety. The decurrent gills are thin, crowded and frequently forked. The slender stem is often off-centre, narrowing to the base, which often curves.

SIZE Cap 3–8 cm, stem 2–5 cm x 5–8 mm.
HABITAT Mostly under conifers. Rarely under elder.
SEASON Late summer to late autumn.
POISONOUS A minority suffer from sickness and hallucinations.
SIMILAR SPECIES Chanterelle (p.167) has a paler, chunkier cap and stem with shallow wrinkles instead of gills. It also has a darker spore colour.

Chanterelle is collected for its culinary value. The convex cap, thick-fleshed and egg-yolk yellow, expands flat and finally funnel-shaped with an inrolled, wavy margin. It has coloured, blunt-edged, deep wrinkles, with cross veins that divide and reunite. These replace the normal gills and run down on to a solid stem. It has a fruity smell.

SIZE Cap 2–10 cm, stem 2–8 cm x 8–20 mm.
HABITAT Under broad-leaved trees (e.g. beech, oak or birch), rarely with conifers; often among moss on sloping ground.
SEASON Summer to autumn.
EDIBLE Mildly peppery taste goes well with egg dishes. Can be eaten raw. Small ones pickle well.
SIMILAR SPECIES See False Chanterelle (p.166).

Cantharellus tubaeformis

This occasional species grows in troops. Previously called *C. infundibuliformis*, it has a depressed, navel-like cap that, unlike Chanterelle, is thin-fleshed, lacks an inrolled margin and is usually yellow-brown. The decurrent, forked wrinkles (in place of gills) start yellow but mature orange-grey and run on to the tall, slender, hollow, flattened, orange-yellow stem. There is little or no smell. Also known as Yellowlegs.

SIZE Cap 2–5 cm, stem 5–8 cm x 5–10 mm.
HABITAT Deciduous and mixed woodland, especially under beech.
SEASON Autumn.
EDIBLE A poorer version of Chanterelle.
SIMILAR SPECIES Yellow forms look like Chanterelle (p.167) but this has a solid stem and fleshier cap.

The cap of this strange fungus is shaped like a trumpet's horn with a split, wavy, rolled edge. The inside is dingy-brown while on the outer (under) surface there are no gills, the black, leathery surface turning pale grey as the spores mature. The stem is merely a hollow extension of the tube-like cap. Also called Trumpet of Death.

SIZE Cap and stem 2–8 cm wide, 4–10 cm tall.
HABITAT In troops or rings, most often in moss under beech.
SEASON Summer to early winter.
EDIBLE A favourite in restaurants where it is served stuffed, but it is leathery and best used dried to add a rich flavour to soups and stews.
SIMILAR SPECIES The rarer *Cantharellus cinereus* differs in producing spores from black, Chanterelle-like wrinkles.

Oyster Mushroom

LENTINACEAE FAMILY

Pleurotus ostreatus

Now widely cultivated. The flat, moist, slate-blue or oyster-coloured caps are fan-shaped with an inrolled margin. They dry grey-buff or cream. Decurrent, crowded, white to pale-straw gills radiate from the point of attachment, where they may fork. Small, lateral stem, downy when young.

SIZE Cap 5–18 cm, stem 2–3 cm x 10–20 mm.
HABITAT In overlapping clusters on living trunks, dead stumps and logs of broad-leaved trees; also on coniferous trees.
SEASON Late autumn and through the winter.
EDIBLE Good flavour and firm-fleshed. Stem region is tougher.
SIMILAR SPECIES *P. pulmonarius* is smaller, with a creamy-white cap. The flesh smells of flour. Usually on beech. See next two pages for species that can be confused with Oyster Mushroom.

The round/oval, creamy-brown caps are darker at the depressed centre. The significant stem is attached nearer to one side of the cap and is almost covered by a continuation of the off-white gills. These regularly fork and reunite over the stem, which fuses with many others at its base. Now rarer due to elm disease.

SIZE Cap 5–12 cm, stem 2–7 cm x 15–30 mm.
HABITAT Clustered on dead elm; also on beech.
SEASON Summer to early autumn.
EDIBLE Tougher and less tasty than Oyster Mushroom.
SIMILAR SPECIES *P. dryinus* on beech and ash has a scaly cap and marginal veil fragments. Oyster Mushroom (p.170) is greyer and lacks the significant branched stem and reuniting gills. It fruits later in the year.

The fan- or kidney-shaped, fleshy cap has an inrolled margin when young. The colour varies; it is initially yellow-orange then olive-green and finally (especially after frost) bronze-brown. It is slimy when moist but dries velvety. The crowded, orange-yellow gills are darker near the short, broad, yellow-brown, felty, lateral stem.

SIZE Cap 3–12 cm, stem 1–2 cm x 10–20 mm.
HABITAT Overlapping tufts on stumps and dead wood of broad-leaved trees, especially beech and birch.
SEASON From late autumn through the winter.
INEDIBLE Slimy cap may cause digestive upset.
SIMILAR SPECIES *P. stipticus* has small, dry, brown caps. Oyster Mushroom has pink spores (p.170).

The Latin genus name refers to the pancake-like shape of this small, bracket-like fungus. The pale-brown, kidney-shaped cap, with a slimy, peelable covering and grooved margin, dries smooth and cream-coloured. The crowded, white gills fan out and turn brown as the spores mature. The stem is lateral or absent.

SIZE Cap 2–7 cm across, (no stem).

HABITAT Overlapping tiers on dead trunks and stumps of broad-leaved trees, especially ash and beech.

SEASON Early summer to late autumn.

INEDIBLE Insubstantial and slimy textured.

SIMILAR SPECIES A number of smaller species grow on fallen twigs, nettles and dead grass stems. Olive Oysterling (p.172) has yellow gills.

This is one of the commonest of a group of grassland fungi with club-shaped fruitbodies the size of a matchstick. The unbranched, orange-yellow club is flattened near the rounded apex and narrows to the base. The spores are borne on the smooth surface.

SIZE 2–6 cm tall, 2–4 mm wide.
HABITAT In short, unimproved grassland. Also among herbs in broad-leaved woods. Solitary or in small groups.
SEASON Midsummer to autumn.
INEDIBLE Insubstantial with a bitter taste.
SIMILAR SPECIES Golden Spindles (*C. fusiformis*), taller and bright yellow, has longer, tufted, bright-yellow clubs. *C. corniculata* has ochre-yellow, coral-like fruit bodies. White Spindles (*Clavaria fragilis*) is white, tufted and unbranched.

Also called *C. cristata*. It has branched, coral-like fruitbodies. This, the commonest species, is usually white, with repeatedly forked, flattened branches ending in pointed, crest-like tips. It is soft and easily broken. Grey/lilac specimens are the result of a fungal infection!

SIZE 2–8 cm tall, 2–6 cm wide.
HABITAT Solitary or gregarious on soil, under broad-leaved trees. Rarely in short turf.
SEASON Midsummer to autumn.
EDIBLE Not recommended as often infected with mould.
SIMILAR SPECIES Grey Coral (p.176). The taller, white Wrinkled Club (*C. rugosa*) is sparsely branched.

This is very similar to the previous species but slightly larger, and the much-branched, coral-like fruitbody is grey-brown. The branches are often flattened and the ends are blunt or rounded but not pointed.

SIZE 3–10 cm tall, 2–8 cm wide.

HABITAT In broad-leaved or mixed woods, usually among leaf litter. Solitary or in small groups.

SEASON Midsummer to late autumn.

EDIBLE Insubstantial and not recommended.

SIMILAR SPECIES Often difficult to separate from Crested Coral (p.175), which usually has pointed branch ends. The rarer *Thelephora palmata* has more purple-brown branches and a strong smell of onion.

Similar in size and appearance to a human brain or cauliflower, the fruitbody is composed of many vertical, flattened, leaf-like lobes. When young and brittle these are cream-coloured with pale-yellow tips but they age brown and tougher. The fleshy basal stem is often partly buried and root-like. It has a slightly sweet smell and tastes of hazelnuts. Also known as Cauliflower Fungus.

SIZE 10–20 cm tall, 15–40 cm wide.

HABITAT On the ground close to living trunks or dead stumps of conifers; mostly with Scots pine.

SEASON Late summer to autumn.

EDIBLE Young, well-washed specimens have a marvellous taste and texture. Must not be eaten when old.

SIMILAR SPECIES Hen of the Woods (p.197) has horizontal lobes with pores on the underside and grows on or near oak.

This species has spines (stalactite-like projections) from the cap in place of gills. It has a medium-sized, fleshy, creamy-buff cap with an inrolled, often wavy or irregular margin. Neighbouring caps may coalesce. The spines are paler than the cap, crowded, brittle and continue on to the top of the short, stocky stem, which is often not centrally attached.

SIZE Cap 3–14 cm, stem 4–6 cm x 15–25 mm.

HABITAT Under both broad-leaved (especially beech) and coniferous trees; often in troops.

SEASON Autumn.

EDIBLE Slightly bitter when raw but excellent after cooking, with a firm texture.

SIMILAR SPECIES The smaller *H. rufescens* has an orange-brown cap.

A curious little fungus growing on old pine cones. The thin, dark-brown cap is shaped like an ear and the convex surface is coarsely velvety and often channelled to the laterally attached stem. In place of gills there are tiny (2–3 mm), grey-brown spines that hang down like stalactites. The slender, cap-coloured stem has a bristly surface.

SIZE Cap 1–2 cm, stem 2–6 cm x 1–2 mm.
HABITAT Singly or in small groups on decaying (often buried) cones of pine.
SEASON Mostly autumn but appearing all year.
INEDIBLE Insubstantial and tough.
SIMILAR SPECIES *Strobilurus esculentus* fruits on spruce cones in the spring; *Baeospora myosura* fruits on a range of cones in autumn. Both have gills, not spines.

With no cap, stem or gills, its fruitbody consists of flattened, soft, grey-brown, fan-shaped lobes that frequently fuse to give a rosette appearance. The lobes are either semi-erect in a shallow bowl-shape, or flat and encrusting twigs and plant stems. The upper surface is radially zoned and felty with a paler, irregularly fringed margin. The smooth, lower, spore-bearing surface is cinnamon-brown and wrinkled.

SIZE In patches, 3–20 cm across.
HABITAT On sandy or acidic soil on heaths, moors and open woodland.
SEASON Summer to late autumn.
INEDIBLE Insubstantial.
SIMILAR SPECIES Hairy Curtain Crust (p.181) grows on wood.

This forms encrustations and rows of small, thin, tough, semicircular, bracket-like caps that frequently fuse with their neighbours. The zoned upper-side is roughly hairy and ranges from yellow-orange to grey-brown (frequently green with algae when old). The paler, broader, undulating margin is hairless. The lower, spore-bearing surface is smooth and initially bright yellow-orange but fades grey-brown. Also called Hairy Stereum.

SIZE Individual caps are 2–6 cm across, 2–3 mm thick.

HABITAT Tiered on stumps, dead standing and fallen wood of broad-leaved trees; also on dead wood on a range of shrubs.

SEASON Throughout the year.

INEDIBLE Tough and leathery.

SIMILAR SPECIES Several 'bleeding' species (p.182). Turkeytail (p.186) has tiny pores on its creamy underside.

Bleeding Broadleaf Crust

Stereum rugosum

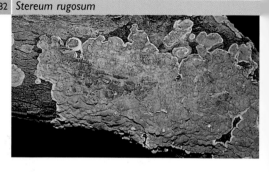

Bleeding Broadleaf Crust is usually found as a hard, flat crust that forms large patches on dead wood. The margins occasionally turn up to form tiny brackets. The pale-ochre surface is initially smooth and flat but becomes uneven and may crack when dry. Fresh specimens bruise red and bleed a red juice when scratched; hence the common name.

SIZE Patches 2–20 cm across, only 1–2 mm thick.
HABITAT Crusts on dead wood of broad-leaved trees, especially hazel and beech.
SEASON Throughout the year.
INEDIBLE Hard and tough.
SIMILAR SPECIES Other bleeders include the red-brown *S. gausapatum* on oak, which regularly forms small brackets; *S. sanguinolentum* grows on coniferous wood.

This species occurs as a flat crust, which turns up to produce small, leathery, bracket-like caps. These have faintly zoned, hairy, pale-grey upper surfaces with pale, undulating margins. When young the underside, like the crust region, is smooth or finely wrinkled and a striking pink-violet colour, fading to dark brown. Previously called *Stereum purpureum*.

SIZE Patches to 15 cm across, brackets 2–4 cm across.
HABITAT Tiered on dead wood of broad-leaved trees. On living wood of rowan and fruit trees, where it causes 'silver leaf' disease. Rarely seen on conifers.
SEASON Throughout the year.
INEDIBLE Very tough.
SIMILAR SPECIES Purplepore Bracket (see p.185) has pores on its under surface and grows on conifers.

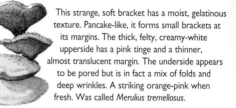

This strange, soft bracket has a moist, gelatinous texture. Pancake-like, it forms small brackets at its margins. The thick, felty, creamy-white upperside has a pink tinge and a thinner, almost translucent margin. The underside appears to be pored but is in fact a mix of folds and deep wrinkles. A striking orange-pink when fresh. Was called *Merulius tremellosus*.

SIZE Individual brackets 2–4 cm across but frequently coalescing.
HABITAT Rotten wood on stumps and fallen trunks. Mostly on broad-leaved trees.
SEASON Commonest in summer and autumn.
INEDIBLE Soft but insubstantial.
SIMILAR SPECIES *Phlebia radiata* (Wrinked Crust) forms soft, bright-orange, radially grooved crusts that grey with age.

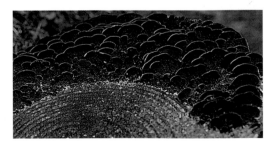

Previously known as *Hirschioporus abietinus*, its small, thin brackets grow in many-layered tiers on dead conifer wood. The upper surface is hairy, grey-brown, undulating, concentrically zoned and grooved. It may turn green from entrapped algae. The margin and pored underside are bright violet when young but fade to chocolate-brown. The pores become more elongated with age.

SIZE Patches to 30 cm x 30 cm. Brackets 2–4 cm aross.
HABITAT Overlapping tiers on dead conifer wood, including sawn logs. Mostly on larch, pine, spruce and fir.
SEASON Throughout the year.
INEDIBLE Insubstantial and tough.
SIMILAR SPECIES The purple-tinged Silverleaf Fungus (p.183) is smooth below and grows on broad-leaved trees.

Turkeytail

Trametes (Coriolus) versicolor

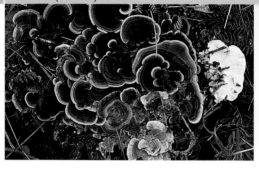

Very common, with semicircular or kidney-shaped, thin, leathery brackets. The upper, wrinkled surface is slightly hairy and shows contrasting concentric zones of black, grey and brown with a paler, undulating margin. The pored underside is creamy-white to pale ochre. Also called Many-zoned Polypore.

SIZE 2–7 cm across, 2–5 cm broad x 1–5 mm thick.
HABITAT On stumps, logs and standing dead wood; also on living wood. Mostly on broad-leaved trees. Usually in large, overlapping groups.
SEASON Throughout the year.
INEDIBLE Like dried leather.
SIMILAR SPECIES The pale-tan *T. hirsuta* is less clearly zoned and more hairy. See also *Stereum hirsutum* (p.181).

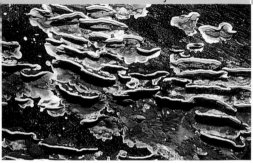

This forms crust-like patches on the underside of branches and overlapping, thin, pliable brackets on upper or vertical surfaces. The grey-brown bracket is faintly zoned, with a whitish margin that ages black, and has an aniseed smell. The pored underside is pale grey, with a white margin but blackens on bruising and with age.

SIZE Brackets 2–6 cm across, 4–7 mm thick.
HABITAT Tiered on dead wood and damaged areas of broad-leaved trees, especially on beech.
SEASON Throughout the year.
INEDIBLE With a leathery texture.
SIMILAR SPECIES The dark-grey pores help distinguish this species from other small brackets, including *B. fumosa*, which has cream-coloured pores and an aniseed smell.

A serious parasite of conifers, especially spruce, the fruitbodies are formed from the lower trunk/upper root zone, where the brackets are often partly hidden by moss and grass. It is crust-like but also produces small, irregular, elongated lobes. These are dark brown to black, with a hard, lumpy surface and a wavy margin showing the white of the underside, which is covered with small, angular pores. If cut open older fruitbodies show annual layers of tubes.

SIZE Up to 15 cm across, 8 cm broad and 4 cm thick.
HABITAT Usually with conifers but also found with heathers.
SEASON Throughout the year as it is perennial.
INEDIBLE Very hard.
SIMILAR SPECIES None in the same habitat.

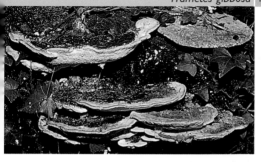

This medium-sized fungus forms semicircular brackets that are much thicker and humped at their point of attachment. The white upper side has a slightly velvety, lumpy surface. Old specimens become browner and are frequently green in the middle from encrusting algae. The creamy-white pores on the underside are unusual in being elongated into thick-walled slots. Was called *Pseudotrametes gibbosa*.

SIZE 10–20 cm across, 6–15 cm broad, 1–5 cm thick.
HABITAT Commonest on dead sycamore and beech.
SEASON Throughout the year.
INEDIBLE Tough even when young.
SIMILAR SPECIES Blushing Bracket (p.190) has a thinner, brown bracket with pores that bruise pink on handling.

A thin-edged bracket with a semicircular-shaped, tough fruitbody with an uneven, concentrically zoned, radially streaked, ochre-brown upper side; paler at the margin. The white underside ages grey-brown but bruises dark pink-red. The large pores are round and angular, some slit-like, others maze-like.

SIZE 4–14 cm across, 4–8 cm broad, 1–3 cm thick.
HABITAT Commonest on willow, birch, hazel, beech and ash.
SEASON Throughout the year.
INEDIBLE Tough, becoming woody.
SIMILAR SPECIES Lumpy Bracket (p.189) also has elongated pores but a whiter, more uneven upperside and it does not flush red when bruised.

Commonest on oak stumps, this hard, corky bracket is unusually thick at its point of attachment. Above it is grey-brown and uneven. Below, the beige pores are greatly elongated (the walls appearing like thick gills) and form a labyrinth or maze-like pattern. (In Greek mythology Daedalus had to find his way through a labyrinth.)

SIZE 8–16 cm across, 4–8 cm broad, 2–5 cm thick.
HABITAT On dead wood of oak; rarely on sweet chestnut.
SEASON Throughout the year.
INEDIBLE Has a very hard texture.
SIMILAR SPECIES The smaller, thinner *Lenzites betulinus* grows mostly on birch. The creamy-ochre underside has much thinner, more regular, gill-like plates.

A very common parasite on birch, which continues to grow on the dead wood. White, smooth and rounded when young, it later develops a convex, kidney or semicircular shape. It is thickest at the lateral point of attachment, which is narrow and stem-like. The white upper side ages brown or grey and often cracks. The margin remains inrolled until maturity. The white underside is punctuated with tiny, round pores. Also known as Razorstrop Fungus.

SIZE 8–30 cm across, 5–20 cm broad, 2–6 cm thick.
HABITAT On trunks and branches of living or dead birch.
SEASON Throughout the year. Fruitbodies persist.
INEDIBLE The tough flesh has a bitter taste.
SIMILAR SPECIES See Hoof Fungus (p.193) – also on birch.

A very hard, broadly attached, perennial fruitbody; successive annual layers of tubes produce a hoof-like shape often as deep as it is wide. The upper side is smooth, pale grey, with darker concentric bands and ridged with concentric furrows. It has a very broad, rounded margin. The underside has minute pores, initially pale grey-brown but later dark brown. The pale-brown, leathery flesh was used when lighting fires; hence its other name – Tinder Fungus.

SIZE 7–40 cm across, 5–20 cm broad, 7–20 cm deep.

HABITAT Mostly on dead or dying birch but also on beech, oak and sycamore.

SEASON Any time – fruitbodies live for many years.

INEDIBLE As tough as the wood it grows on!

SIMILAR SPECIES *Phellinus igniarius* has a black, cracked 'hoof' and rusty-brown flesh. Occasional, mostly on willow.

More like an ox tongue in shape, colour and texture, this strange fungus is soft and moist when young, with a rough, pinky-red upper side and a broad margin. Older ones are firmer, smooth and liver-brown with a sharper edge. The straw-yellow pores bruise and age red-brown, often exuding a blood-red juice. The watery tubes are readily separated from the thick flesh, which has the appearance of raw steak.

SIZE 8–20 cm across, 3–6 cm thick.

HABITAT Usually low on the trunk of old, living oak and sweet chestnut trees; also on their stumps.

SEASON Late summer to autumn; not persisting.

EDIBLE Best simmered; it can be bitter.

SIMILAR SPECIES None.

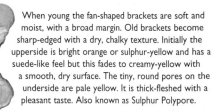

When young the fan-shaped brackets are soft and moist, with a broad margin. Old brackets become sharp-edged with a dry, chalky texture. Initially the upperside is bright orange or sulphur-yellow and has a suede-like feel but this fades to creamy-yellow with a smooth, dry surface. The tiny, round pores on the underside are pale yellow. It is thick-fleshed with a pleasant taste. Also known as Sulphur Polypore.

SIZE Individual caps 5–20 cm across, 2–6 cm thick.
HABITAT Tiered on oak, sweet chestnut, yew and beech.
SEASON Summer to early autumn. Occasionally persisting.
EDIBLE Texture of chicken but can cause nausea or rash.
SIMILAR SPECIES Pale specimens of Giant Polypore (p.196) look similar but the pores bruise black.

Giant Polypore

Meripilus giganteus

Produces clusters of overlapping brackets up to a metre across.
Each fan-shaped lobe arises from a common bulbous base. Tan-
brown, radially wrinkled and faintly zoned with fine, darker-
brown fibres. The undulating, thin margin often divides
into smaller sub-brackets. The small-pored, cream
underside blackens on handling, as does the flesh.

SIZE Lobes 10–35 cm across, 1–3 cm thick.
HABITAT On stumps, roots or near the base
of living broad-leaved trees; mostly on beech.
SEASON Summer to early autumn. Soon rotting.
EDIBLE Slow-cooked young brackets are edible but can
cause gastric upset in some people.
SIMILAR SPECIES Confusable with Chicken of the Woods
(p.195), Hen of the Woods (p.197) and Dryad's Saddle (p.199).

Typically found at the base of oak, it forms a cauliflower-like rosette of small, soft, horizontal, grey-brown, leafy brackets that branch from a central white stem. Each thin, undulating, fan-shaped segment is radially furrowed. The small, round pores on the underside continue to the top of the stem. The sweet smell becomes less pleasant as it ages.

SIZE Whole fruitbody up to 40 cm in diameter.
HABITAT On stumps, roots and at the base of living broad-leaved trees; mostly with oak.
SEASON Autumn. Not persisting.
EDIBLE Slow cooking softens the tough texture.
SIMILAR SPECIES Has been confused with Giant Polypore (p.196) and Wood Cauliflower (p.177) – the latter grows at the base of conifers.

The mature fruitbody is shaped like a broad, inverted cone. The flat top is initially rusty-orange, convex and concentrically grooved. It is soft and spongy when young, with a fuzzy, mat-like surface. It ages dry, dark red-brown to black with a paler edge. The olive-yellow pores (left of photo) become maze-like and turn brown with age and handling. The tubes run on to the stocky brown stem. Produces a yellow/brown/red dye.

SIZE Cap 8–30 cm diameter, stem 3–8 cm x 2–6 cm.
HABITAT On conifer roots/stumps; rare with birch.
SEASON Autumn. Dried specimens persist into winter.
INEDIBLE Often encrusts old pine needles.
SIMILAR SPECIES None.

The large cap is semicircular or saddle-shaped (in Greek mythology dryads were wood nymphs), occasionally circular. It is flat-topped or depressed near the lateral or off-centred stem. The upper side is tan-yellow with concentric bands of dark-brown, flat scales. The underside has large, angular, creamy-yellow pores. The tubes run on to the thick stem, which has a brown-black, velvety base.

SIZE Cap to 50 cm x 5 cm thick,
stem 3–10 cm x 1–6 cm.
HABITAT Solitary or tiered on dying/dead
wood, especially with beech, ash and sycamore;
rare on conifers.
SEASON Spring to summer. Not persisting.
EDIBLE Edges of young caps are the most tender.
SIMILAR SPECIES Winter-fruiting *P. brumalis* has a
mushroom-shaped, small cap. It grows on fallen branches.

Growing on the ground, this species is easy to mistake for a toadstool but it has a thin, tough, corky cap with tubes on its underside. The circular cap is flat or funnel-shaped and velvety, with concentric yellow-brown, rust and grey-brown bands that give the appearance of tree rings. The pale, thin, undulating edge often splits. The pores are rusty-brown, angular and decurrent on to the narrow, frequently flattened, velvety, brown stem.

SIZE Cap 3–7 cm, stem 2–5 cm x 3–8 mm.
HABITAT On well-drained or burnt ground; often under pine, and with heather and gorse.
SEASON Late summer but old fruitbodies persist.
INEDIBLE However, it is used in floral decorations.
SIMILAR SPECIES Winter Polypore (*Polyporus brumalis*) lacks the concentric zones and grows on dead wood.

The thick, broad-edged, semicircular brackets have a red-brown
(later black), coarsely hairy upper side. The margin remains a
brighter, yellow-brown colour. The underside is pale yellow,
maturing brown, with small pores that often exude clear,
dew-like drops. The cap is soft and moist when
young; it dries tougher.

SIZE 10–25 cm across, 8–20 cm broad,
4–10 cm thick.
HABITAT Solitary or in small groups on tree
trunks; most frequently on ash and apple.
SEASON Summer but persisting through the year.
INEDIBLE Tough and often insect-ridden.
SIMILAR SPECIES *I. dryadeus* grows near the base of
oak and the non-shaggy bracket exudes orange-red droplets.

Southern Bracket

GANODERMACEAE FAMILY

Ganoderma australe (adspersum)

The very woody, perennial brackets consist of several layers of tubes; the lower layers are broader than the upper, above which is thick, dark-brown flesh. The upper side is crust-like, with dark-brown bumps and concentric ridges. The edge is rounded. The tiny, creamy-grey pores on the underside bruise brown when scratched.

SIZE 10–30 cm across, 10–25 cm broad, 4–8 cm thick.
HABITAT Near the base of living trunks and dead stumps; commonest on beech, recorded on a wide range of broad-leaved trees and shrubs.
SEASON All year, as the brackets are perennial.
INEDIBLE As hard as wood.
SIMILAR SPECIES Much confused with *G. applanatum*, which is more sharp-edged and has thin, white-flecked, brown flesh.

Judas is said to have hanged himself on an elder, the commonest host of this fungus traditionally known as Jew's Ear. Initially cup-shaped and smooth, the fruitbody elongates to the shape of a wrinkled human ear. When moist it is soft, gelatinous and date-brown but it dries smaller, darker and hard. The upper (outer) surface is slightly velvety. It is attached laterally by a small stalk.

SIZE 2–7 cm across and 2–5 cm broad.
HABITAT Common on living or dead wood of elder. Also recorded on many other woody species.
SEASON Throughout the year, softening after rain.
EDIBLE Best in soups or stews; not easily fried.
SIMILAR SPECIES *A. mesenterica* (Tripe Fungus) is like a small, hairy bracket above but is gelatinous below. On stumps/dead wood; not on elder.

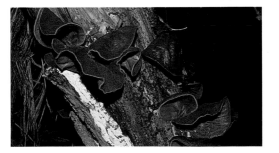

Yellow Brain

Tremella mesenterica

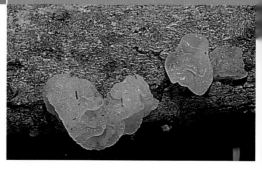

This curious fungus is easy to spot after wet weather with its bright, yellow-orange colour and very soft, shiny, irregularly folded, gelatinous fruitbody. Originally disc-like, it soon becomes more brain-shaped. Attached to pieces of dead wood by a relatively small basal area; when knocked it wobbles like jelly. In dry weather it shrinks, darkens, becomes very hard and is more difficult to find.

SIZE 2–8 cm across.

HABITAT On dead twigs and branches of broad-leaved trees, especially hazel, birch and ash. Also on gorse.

SEASON All year but more frequent in winter.

INEDIBLE Insubstantial, with an odd texture.

SIMILAR SPECIES Leafy Brain (*T. foliacea*) is date-brown and has leaf-like, undulating lobes.

When growing on fallen branches the gelatinous black fruitbody is disc- or top-shaped and attached by a short stalk; on erect branches it is more bracket-like and stalkless. It becomes lobed and brain-like when mature. The upper side is roughened with tiny warts, the sides and lower surface are slightly downy. It shrinks to a hard, black crust when dry.

SIZE 1–5 cm across.

HABITAT Grouped on dead wood, including stumps of broad-leaved trees; most frequent on oak, beech and hazel.

SEASON Throughout the year.

INEDIBLE It has an odd, slippery texture.

SIMILAR SPECIES The firmer Black Bulgar (p.239) leaves a black mark when rubbed with a finger.

Dacrymyces stillatus

Each rounded, soft fruitbody is only a few mm across but this species grows in large groups and is easily seen. Neighbouring fruitbodies often merge. It occurs as both an orange and a paler yellow form. When old it dries harder and darker.

SIZE 2–5 mm across.

HABITAT On dead wood of both broad-leaved and coniferous trees. Especially common on wooden gates, fence-posts and greenhouses after rain.

SEASON
Throughout the year.

INEDIBLE
Insubstantial.

SIMILAR SPECIES
Can be confused with Coral Spot (p.231), which also produces many tiny, rounded fruitbodies on dead wood. These are dry, warty and pink or dark-red; not orange.

Gelatinous in texture, the tiny, yellow, smooth, cylindrical fruitbodies turn orange on drying. Most are simple and finger-like but some branch near the apex. Shiny when moist, they are erect and usually gregarious; growing in lines or as groups of 4 or 5 together in a hand-like cluster.

SIZE 2–10 mm high x 1–2 mm wide.
HABITAT On dead wood of broad-leaved trees, especially where the bark has been lost. Also on conifers.
SEASON Throughout the year.
INEDIBLE Insubstantial and surprisingly tough.
SIMILAR SPECIES *C. furcata* is externally very similar but it grows on dead conifers. See Pale Stagshorn (p.208).

Pale Stagshorn

DACRYMYCETACEAE FAMILY

Calocera pallidospathulata

This species is rarely mentioned in older books on fungal identification because it is a relative newcomer to Great Britain; the first record, near Pickering, was in 1969. It is now very common, however, especially in conifer plantations, where it frequently takes the place of Small Stagshorn, from which it differs in having a paler, larger, stalked, more flattened, club-shaped fruitbody.

SIZE 5–15 mm high x 2–4 mm wide.
HABITAT Gregarious on dead conifers and other woody species.
SEASON Throughout the year.
INEDIBLE Slimy texture.
SIMILAR SPECIES The more slender Small Stagshorn (p.207) grows mainly on the dead wood of broad-leaved trees.

This beautiful, bright golden-yellow to orange fungus has a gelatinous, tough texture and is smooth and shiny when moist. Firmly rooted in the dead wood from which it grows, the base is paler, flattened and frequently fused with neighbouring fruitbodies. The forked, cylindrical branches end in pointed tips that are sometimes further branched, as in antlers.

SIZE 3–8 cm high, 2–3 cm wide.
HABITAT On stumps and dead roots of conifers, most frequent on pine.
SEASON Autumn.
INEDIBLE Tough and tasteless.
SIMILAR SPECIES Other *Calocera* species are smaller and less branched. Coral fungi (pp.175 & 176) are dry and brittle.

This is one of our largest fungi, similar in size and shape to a football. The solid, young fruitbodies have a thin, white, smooth, dry skin that later turns olive and finally brown when it splits open. The mushroom-smelling flesh is white and firm but turns olive-yellow and later brown and powdery as the spores develop.

SIZE 20–75 cm diameter when mature.

HABITAT Occasional in pasture, woods and gardens; often with nettles on rubbish tips. In groups; forms rings.

SEASON Early summer to autumn. Old ones persist.

EDIBLE When still white inside it is excellent; best baked or fried with lemon juice to add flavour.

SIMILAR SPECIES See Mosaic Puffball (p.211).

This puffball is the size of a large tennis ball; with a flattened top and a two-layered skin. The rough, white outer skin cracks into pyramid-shaped warts but these soon disappear to reveal a white inner skin patterned with a honeycomb-like mosaic. Later smooth and brown, when a hole appears and the edges spread back to release the brown spores. The leathery, non-fertile base persists like a thick saucer.

SIZE 5–15 cm diameter.
HABITAT In small groups on unimproved upland pasture. More frequent in the north.
SEASON Summer to autumn. Brown basal region persists over winter.
EDIBLE The inner flesh must be still white.
SIMILAR SPECIES Small specimens of Giant Puffball (p.210) have a single smooth skin and no infertile base.

This has a long, thick stalk region below the spherical apex, giving it a pestle or drum-stick shape. The white flesh is protected by a creamy-brown skin covered with tiny spines and granules. These are soon lost, revealing the brown, parchment-like inner skin, which splits at the apex and peels open, releasing brown spores. The non-fertile, wrinkled stalk region persists after the spores have been shed.

SIZE 8–15 cm high, apex 5–10 cm, stalk 3–5 cm across.
HABITAT In parkland, open broad-leaved woodland and on heaths. Occasional; solitary or in small groups.
SEASON Late summer to autumn.
EDIBLE Young specimens are edible.
SIMILAR SPECIES See Common Puffball (p.213).

The globular head region is often flattened but narrows abrubtly to a stem region that is about half the total height. Initially the skin is covered in creamy-white, conical warts on the head region but these fall off, leaving a mesh-like pattern on a brown, paper-like skin. This ruptures to form a small apical pore through which the spores escape. Young specimens are firm and white inside.

SIZE 2–5 cm diameter, 3–8 cm tall.

HABITAT On soil or decayed wood in both broad-leaved and coniferous woods. Also on woodchip. Usually gregarious.

SEASON Late summer to autumn.

EDIBLE Only edible when firm and young.

SIMILAR SPECIES The smaller Stump Puffball (p.216) lacks the patterned surface.

Dusky Puffball

Lycoperdon nigrescens

Shaped like a rounded spinning top, it differs when young from Common Puffball (p.213) in being covered with pale-brown, short spines, groups of which converge like wigwam poles. These later fall off, leaving a mesh-like pattern on a brown background. Initially firm and white inside it becomes olive-brown as the spores mature and are released through a small apical pore. It has an unpleasant odour when young, hence its former name *L. foetidum*.

SIZE 2–5 cm diameter, 2–4 cm high.

HABITAT Frequent in acid woodlands and heaths.

SEASON Summer to autumn.

INEDIBLE Unpleasant smell is offputting.

SIMILAR SPECIES Spiny Puffball (p.215) has longer spines and a darker spore mass. See Common Puffball (p.213).

Dusky Puffball (p.214) is often wrongly recorded as Spiny Puffball, which is pear-shaped with a globular apex and short, conical stalk. Even young specimens are dark and densely covered with long brown spines, groups of which curve and fuse at the top to form little pyramids (3–4 mm high). These later fall off, leaving a net-like pattern on the dark-brown skin. At maturity the spore mass becomes dark brown. A small round pore opens at the apex.

SIZE 2–6 cm diameter, 3–7 cm high.
HABITAT In broad-leaved woods (e.g. beech) on chalk. Commonest in S. England.
SEASON Late summer to autumn.
INEDIBLE Not worth eating.
SIMILAR SPECIES See Dusky Puffball (p.214).

This puffball grows in large clusters on rotting wood (this includes dead roots, when it appears to grow on soil). Pear-shaped, and often attached by white strands, it starts granular and creamy-white but matures smooth and ochre-brown, when a small hole opens at the apex. When young the inside is firm and white; the upper area turns olive-brown as the spores mature.

SIZE 1–4 cm diameter, 1–6 cm high.
HABITAT Clustered on rotting wood of both broad-leaved and coniferous trees. Very common.
SEASON Summer to late autumn. Old ones persist.
EDIBLE Can be eaten young but has an unpleasant odour.
SIMILAR SPECIES Common Puffball (p.213) can grow on wood.

One of the commonest puffballs in short grass, it is broadly pear-shaped and flattened at the apex. It is often wider than it is tall and the base is barely narrower. When young the white skin is granular but the granules wash off in the rain leaving a smooth, pale-brown surface. Inside, the olive-brown spore mass is clearly separated from the white, lower, non-fertile region by a membrane. The spores escape through a large apical hole.

SIZE 2–5 cm diameter, 2–4 cm high.
HABITAT Gregarious in lawns, heaths and near the sea.
SEASON Summer to autumn. Lower region persists.
EDIBLE Only edible when the flesh is white.
SIMILAR SPECIES The distinct membrane between the fertile and non-fertile region prevents confusion with other puffballs.

The size and shape of a small golf ball, the smooth, white outer skin splits and falls away, revealing a thin, lead-grey (hence *plumbea*), parchment-like inner skin. This matures dark brown and peels open, revealing the red-brown spore mass that fills the entire fruitbody. When young the inside is firm and white. The fruitbody is attached to the ground at a very small point of contact. Older ones become detached and roll around.

SIZE 2–4 cm diameter.
HABITAT Short grass, including golf courses.
SEASON Late summer to autumn.
EDIBLE Young ones provide a mouthful each.
SIMILAR SPECIES The larger Brown Puffball (*B. nigrescens*) matures a shiny purple-black. More common in the north.

Spherical or slightly flattened, Common Earthball may become slightly lobed. The tiny, stalk-like region is often buried in the soil. The yellow-brown, thick (to 5 mm), scaly skin has a reptilian appearance and finally ruptures to release the spores. Initially white, the inside is soon purple-black with white streaks and finally develops into a powdery, brown spore mass. It has a rubbery smell.

SIZE 3–10 cm diameter.

HABITAT On the ground near trees, especially birch and oak; prefers acid soils. Even grows in pavements.

SEASON Summer to autumn. Old ones persist a few months.

POISONOUS Causes gastric upset, especially if undercooked.

SIMILAR SPECIES See Scaly Earthball (p.220).

This has a more pear-shaped fruitbody, which has a distinct, grooved, stalk-like base attached to white threads. The tough, leathery skin is thinner (2–3 mm) than that of Common Earthball and has much finer, brown scales (these are lost in old specimens). The skin ruptures near the apex to produce an irregularly shaped opening. Initially white then dark brown and marbled, the inside finally develops into a brown spore mass. The smell is indistinct.

SIZE 3–5 cm diameter, 6–7 cm high.
HABITAT On acid soils in woods and on heathland.
SEASON Summer to autumn.
POISONOUS Not deadly but can cause diarrhoea.
SIMILAR SPECIES See Common Earthball
(p.219). Puffballs (pp. 210–218) have thinner,
softer skins.

The immature stage ('Witch's Egg') feels soft, due to a jelly-like layer just beneath the surface. This later splits at the apex and a thick, white, hollow stem emerges with the texture of polystyrene and bearing a wrinkled, conical, slimy, olive-green head topped by a small white ring. At this stage the fungus smells like bad drains and attracts flies, which eat the spore-bearing slime, leaving a white honeycomb top.

SIZE 'Egg' 3–5 cm diameter. Mature 10–20 cm x 2–3 cm.

HABITAT Among leaf litter in woodlands, also in gardens.

SEASON Early summer to late autumn.

EDIBLE The egg stage (before it smells) can be eaten. Said to be an aphrodisiac!

SIMILAR SPECIES The 'egg' looks like a puffball. *P. hadriani* on sand dunes has a lilac-pink egg.

Less common than Stinkhorn but still frequent, the Dog Stinkhorn is much smaller and the more elongated white egg stage is tinged pale brown. The slim, brittle, polystyrene-like stem is white in the lower regions but dark orange near the apex, which bears the pointed, dark-olive, slimy spore mass. A mildly unpleasant smell attracts flies, which eat the spore layer, leaving a dark-orange honeycomb at the tip.

SIZE 'Egg' 2–3 cm diameter.
Mature 4–8 cm x 1 cm.

HABITAT In woodland leaf litter and around rotting wood.

SEASON Summer to autumn.

INEDIBLE The egg is too small to be worthwhile.

SIMILAR SPECIES The small size and orange tip distinguishes it from Stinkhorn (p.221).

Earthstars are like puffballs with an outer skin that splits and peels back. None are common but this one is locally frequent. Initially like a pointed puffball, the thick (to 5 mm), fleshy outer skin splits into 5 or 6 creamy-brown lobes that open flat in a star-like pattern. The base of each lobe splits to form a raised circular collar. This surrounds the thin-skinned inner bag, which has a small fringed apical opening through which the spores escape.

SIZE 4–7 cm diameter (when fully open).
HABITAT Among leaf litter of broad-leaved trees.
SEASON Late summer to autumn.
INEDIBLE Tough and full of spores.
SIMILAR SPECIES The flesh-coloured
G. rufescens lacks a collar. *G. pectinatum*
has a stalked inner bag.

Bird's Nest fungi are very small. This is the commonest, with a deeply cup-shaped fruitbody, the opening of which is initially covered by a white skin that ruptures to reveal a group of tiny, grey, egg-shaped sacs (peridioles) containing the spores. Each is attached by a thin thread. The inner surface of the 'nest' is grooved and grey. The outer surface is red-brown and bristly.

SIZE 1.5 cm tall, 1 cm diameter.
HABITAT On dead twigs, needles and bark fragments.
SEASON Summer to early autumn.
INEDIBLE Tough and tiny.
SIMILAR SPECIES On woodchip *C. olla* has a smooth outer side and a trumpet-shaped top. *Crucibulum laeve* has smooth, straight-edged 'nests'.

At a casual glance this looks like a piece of orange peel. Initially bowl-like, the thin-fleshed, fragile fruitbody expands to a saucer-shape and may flatten but it has an irregular, undulating margin that is frequently split. The inner, spore-bearing surface is smooth and bright orange; the outer surface is minutely downy and paler. There is no stalk.

SIZE 2–8 cm diameter.

HABITAT Gregarious on damp, bare soil, occasionally among herbs in shady places. Commonest on woodland rides, ditch banks and in gardens.

SEASON Autumn to early winter.

EDIBLE Needs cooking; bland flavour.

SIMILAR SPECIES The vivid-red Scarlet Elfcup (*Sarcoscypha austriaca*) grows on fallen twigs.

Young fruitbodies start saucer-shaped but one side develops faster, causing it to elongate, split and curl inwards. This gives rise to its English name – Hare's Ear. The ochre-yellow outer surface is smooth. The short, white stalk region is usually buried in woodland soil.

SIZE 2–5 cm across, 4–10 cm high.
HABITAT Gregarious among leaf litter or moss under beech or oak. Occasional.
SEASON Summer to autumn.
EDIBLE Insubstantial and not recommended.
SIMILAR SPECIES Tan Ear (*O. alutacea*) has a paler outer surface and is more cup-shaped.

The flattened, saucer-like fruitbody is much smaller than those of the *Peziza* genus but the clustered nature and scarlet colour of Common Eyelash make it easy to find. Starting knob-like then saucer-shaped, the fruitbody finally flattens but maintains a small, upturned margin. The bright-scarlet, smooth inner surface contrasts with the brown, bristly hairs of the outer side; these project above the margin like eyelashes. There is no stalk.

SIZE 0.5–1.5 cm diameter.

HABITAT Clustered on damp, rotting wood and on damp soil.

SEASON Spring to late autumn.

INEDIBLE Insubstantial.

SIMILAR SPECIES Several closely related species are only separated by microscopic features.

The genus *Peziza* contains many medium-sized, thin and fragile species with a cup- or saucer-shaped fruitbody and little or no stalk. *P. badia* is one of the largest, and the undulating, irregular fruitbody lacks a stalk. The smooth, inner, spore-bearing surface is dark olive-brown; the outer is slightly scurfy near the margin and deep red-brown.

SIZE 3–8 cm diameter.
HABITAT Gregarious on moist, acid soil, especially on paths and ditch banks.
SEASON Late summer to autumn.
POISONOUS Especially if eaten raw.
SIMILAR SPECIES Most other *Peziza* species are a paler colour on one or both surfaces. See pp. 229 & 230.

Much paler than the previous species, this has large, shallow, saucer-like fruitbodies and an undulating margin that is frequently split, giving a toothed appearance. There is no stalk. The smooth, inner, spore-bearing surface is a pale chestnut-brown, contrasting with the pale cream of the scurfy outer surface.

SIZE 3–12 cm diameter.

HABITAT On the ground, often close to rotting stumps. Also on sawdust.

SEASON Early summer to autumn.

INEDIBLE Related species are poisonous.

SIMILAR SPECIES The fawn-coloured Blistered Cup (p.230) is most easily separated by its habitat. *P. succosa* is darker brown and exudes a yellow juice when broken.

The young fruitbody is deeply cup-shaped with only a small central opening but this enlarges as the fungus grows. The margins remain inrolled but become split, resulting in a ragged appearance. The inner surface is pale brown, and smooth but wrinkled; the outer side is scurfy and pale buff. Neighbouring fruitbodies often fuse to form large clusters.

SIZE 3–8 cm diameter.
HABITAT Old straw bales, manure, horse dung, cultivated mushroom beds, compost heaps and rich soil.
SEASON Throughout the year.
POISONOUS Edible if well cooked but not recommended.
SIMILAR SPECIES The smaller *P. cerea* grows on damp mortar, sand bags and soil, especially in poorly ventilated cellars.

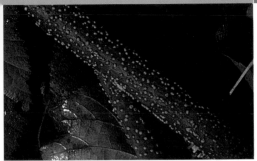

Gregarious on small, dead twigs or other wood, where the hundreds of minute, cushion-like, soft fruitbodies may almost cover the surface. Most commonly found is the pale orange-pink, non-sexual form. The true sexual form is dark red or red-brown, with a bumpy surface shaped like a tiny raspberry. Both forms occasionally grow together.

SIZE 0.5–1.0 mm diameter.
HABITAT Usually on dead branches and twigs of broad-leaved trees and shrubs. Often on wood piles.
SEASON Throughout the year.
INEDIBLE Insubstantial.
SIMILAR SPECIES Common Jellyspot (p.206) produces hundreds of tiny fruitbodies on dead wood, but when fresh these are very soft and orange in colour.

White Saddle

HELVELLACEAE FAMILY

Helvella crispa

This odd-looking fungus has a saddle-shaped cap with two or three undulating, irregular lobes and margins free of the stalk. The upper, spore-bearing surface is creamy-white; the lower surface is pale ochre and slightly downy. The stem is brittle, white and internally chambered with deep, longitudinal surface furrows, some of which fork and reunite.

SIZE Cap 2–6 cm, stem 4–7 cm x 2–4 cm.
HABITAT Under broad-leaved trees and beside woodland paths.
SEASON Summer to autumn.
POISONOUS Can cause gastric upset, especially if eaten raw.
SIMILAR SPECIES Elfin Saddle (p.233) has a dark-grey, more convoluted cap. Morel (p.235) has a brain-like cap and a smoother stem.

This is like a dark-coloured version of the preceding species. The cap is more convoluted and the irregular lobes have rounded margins that are attached to the stem, resulting in hollow chambers. The cap is dark grey to black on the outside and a similar colour within the chambers. The grey-brown, hollow stalk is deeply furrowed and has numerous cross walls.

SIZE Cap 2–4 cm, stem 2–5 cm x 1–2 cm.
HABITAT On sandy or burnt ground under both coniferous and broad-leaved trees.
SEASON Summer to autumn.
POISONOUS Can cause gastric upset so best avoided.
SIMILAR SPECIES White Saddle (p.232) is much paler and the cap lobes are free of the stem.

False Morel

DISCINACEAE FAMILY

Gyromitra esculenta

Also known as Turban Fungus, this is uncommon in Britain but can be mistaken for Morel (p.235) and is deadly poisonous. The broad, fist-shaped, deeply lobed, brain-like, red-brown cap is divided internally into a number of hollow chambers. The short, creamy-brown stem is externally furrowed and internally hollowed into several chambers. It is fragile in texture.

SIZE Cap 5–15 cm, stem 2–5 cm x 2–3 cm.
HABITAT In coniferous woods. Less rare in Scotland.
SEASON Spring to early summer.
POISONOUS Can be fatal and even when consumed after careful preparation is suspected of causing cancer.
SIMILAR SPECIES See Morel (p.235).

The hollow, egg-shaped cap may be globular or more
conical and is often not symmetrical. The deeply pitted
surface is like honeycomb and the pits vary from pale
brown to grey; darker when old. The pale-ochre stem
is grooved near its base and has a single hollow
chamber.

SIZE Cap 3–8 cm across, stem 3–8 cm x 1.5–2.5 cm.

HABITAT On well-drained soil, usually under broad-
leaved trees in woodland edges, hedgerows and gardens.

SEASON April to May with a short fruiting season.

EDIBLE Wonderful flavour and texture. Dries well.

SIMILAR SPECIES *M. elata* has a dark-brown, pointed, conical cap
with the pits in vertical rows. See False Morel (p.234).

Jellybaby

LEOTIACEAE FAMILY

Leotia lubrica

A distinctive little fungus with a slippery, gelatinous feel, its rounded olive-yellow cap becomes flat and centrally depressed but with inrolled, lobed margins and a smooth underside. The pale-yellow stem is slightly flattened and flecked with tiny green specks.

SIZE Cap 1–1.5 cm across, stem 2–5 cm x 4–7 mm.
HABITAT In moist, bare ground and among moss under broad-leaved trees, especially beech.
SEASON Late summer to autumn.
INEDIBLE Insubstantial.
SIMILAR SPECIES The rarer, yellow, tongue-like *Spathularia flavida* grows under conifers. *Mitrula paludosa*, which grows in waterlogged leaf litter, has a club-shaped, orange head and a slender, white stem.

Wood that has been stained blue-green by the action of this fungus is commonly found; the fruitbodies are rarer. Initially goblet-shaped with a short stalk, the top becomes saucer-shaped and later irregularly wavy. The smooth upper surface is bright blue-green; the outer surface and stalk start paler but mature blue-green. It is soft in texture. Formerly known as *Chlorosplenium aeruginascens*.

SIZE 0.5–1.0 cm diameter.
HABITAT On dead wood of broad-leaved trees, e.g. oak.
SEASON From spring to autumn.
INEDIBLE The stained wood is part of the intricate patterns displayed in Tunbridge ware.
SIMILAR SPECIES None.

The soft, jelly-like consistency is similar to that of the basidiomycete Jelly Fungi (pp.203–209). The tiny, purple-pink, spherical fruitbody becomes more like an inverted cone with a smooth, flat disc or saucer-shaped top and a very short stalk. The disc edges are wavy and frequently distorted by the proximity of neighbouring fruitbodies. Formerly known as *Coryne sarcoides*.

SIZE 0.5–1.5 cm diameter.
HABITAT Gregarious. Clustered on barkless dead wood of broad-leaved trees, especially beech.
SEASON Most frequent in autumn and winter.
INEDIBLE Insubstantial.
SIMILAR SPECIES The larger *A. cylichnium* is more cup-shaped. *Neobulgaria pura* is a pale flesh colour.

This species has a firm, rubbery consistency. Top-shaped with
inrolled margins, it later flattens to become more like a thick button
with a concave, shiny-black upper surface that leaves a black mark
when rubbed with a finger. The outer surface is scurfy and dark
brown. In dry conditions the shrunken fruitbody has a leathery feel.

SIZE 1–3 cm diameter, 1–1.5 cm high.
HABITAT Gregarious, sometimes clustered.
Grows from the bark of fallen trunks, mostly
of oak and sweet chestnut.
SEASON Autumn and into early winter.
INEDIBLE Like eating rubber!
SIMILAR SPECIES Witches' Butter (p.205) is
less firm, has a warty surface and does not leave a
black mark.

Hairy Earthtongue

GEOGLOSSACEAE FAMILY

Trichoglossum hirsutum

The dark-brown to black fruitbody is not much bigger than a matchstick. It is club-shaped with a smooth, flattened, tongue-like, fertile head region that narrows abruptly to a more cylindrical, velvety stem.

SIZE 3–8 cm tall.
HABITAT Among moss in wet, acid, unimproved grassland and especially with bog moss (*Sphagnum*).
SEASON Late summer to autumn.
INEDIBLE Insubstantial.
SIMILAR SPECIES On sandy soils the Smooth Earthtongue (*Geoglossum cookeanum*) is smaller, with a less distinct head region and smooth stem. The less common Green Earthtongue (*Microglossum viride*) grows on mossy woodland banks.

The tiny, finger-like fruitbodies stand out because of their bright colour. The lower part is cylindrical, smooth and curving; it merges into the slightly broader, rough-surfaced, fertile apex. They grow from buried dead caterpillars or pupae of butterflies and moths.

SIZE 2–5 cm high, 0.5 cm wide.

HABITAT Solitary or in small groups, emerging from a shallowly buried larva or pupa that the fungus has killed. In grassland or among woodland leaf litter.

SEASON Late summer to late autumn.

INEDIBLE Related species used in Chinese medicine.

SIMILAR SPECIES The yellow-brown *C. ophioglossoides* parasitises the False Truffle (p.244). See also the smooth-surfaced Yellow Club (p.174).

Autumnal inspection of grass flower heads may reveal a small, brown-black, hard, banana-shaped object. This Ergot sclerotium (resting stage) falls to the ground and produces tiny, drumstick-shaped fruitbodies in spring (see inset). These bear sticky spores that infect grasses (and cereals) via their stigmas and take over the flower to produce a sclerotium, which is the cause of ergotism from contaminated flour.

SIZE Sclerotium varies with host: 5–20 mm x 2–4 mm.

HABITAT On the flowers of grasses and cereals.

SEASON Late summer to autumn.

POISONOUS Used medicinally to prevent haemorrhage after childbirth and to ease migraine.

SIMILAR SPECIES None.

Although not as prized as species found in France and Italy, this is once again being collected in Britain by truffle hunters. It is about the size, shape and colour of a squash ball but covered with pyramid-shaped warts, thus looking like a rounded pine cone. The inside is pale brown, marbled white, with a strong but pleasant smell and a nutty taste.

SIZE 3–7 cm in diameter.
HABITAT Buried in the ground under broad-leaved trees; mostly under beech on chalky soil.

SEASON Spring, summer and autumn.
EDIBLE Small amounts are used as flavouring.
SIMILAR SPECIES The much more valuable Perigord or Black Truffle (*T. melanosporum*) has grooved polygonal warts but is not found in Britain in the wild.

False Truffle

Elaphomyces granulatus

This is one of the most frequently found of the subterranean fungi
as it is occasionally parasitised by a club-shaped fungus, *Cordyceps
ophioglossoides*, which emerges above ground. Firm and about the
size and shape of a large marble, its thick, warty, red-brown skin
surrounds the flecked, purple-brown flesh that darkens as the
spores mature. Also known as Hart's Truffle.

SIZE 2–4 cm diameter.
HABITAT Just below the leaf-litter layer in mixed and
coniferous woodland.
SEASON Throughout the year.
INEDIBLE Has been used to adulterate edible
truffles.
SIMILAR SPECIES The very similar *E. muricatus* has a
much thicker skin surrounding the central spore region.

One of the commonest wood-rotting fungi. The small, erect, tough fruitbody is simple and finger-shaped or more often strap-like and forked at its apex, giving it an antler shape. It is also known as Stag's Horn Fungus. Typically black and downy near the base but grey-white on the upper regions; it becomes all black and warty during the winter.

SIZE 3–5 cm high, stalk region 2–5 mm wide.
HABITAT Dead wood, especially on rotting stumps of broad-leaved trees. Rarely on conifers.
SEASON Throughout the year.
INEDIBLE It is very tough.
SIMILAR SPECIES *X. carpophila* is more slender, less branched and grows among leaf litter on old beech fruits.

As its name implies, the clusters of hard, warty, finger-like fruitbodies are distinctly macabre in appearance. Initially grey-brown or brown, the upper region is swollen, flattened and occasionally lobed; it tapers to a short, similar-coloured stalk region. The inside is firm and white under the black, outer, spore-bearing layer.

SIZE 3–7 cm high, 1–3 cm wide.
HABITAT On or near old stumps; usually on beech.
SEASON Summer through to spring. Old ones persist.
INEDIBLE Very hard.
SIMILAR SPECIES *X. longipes* has much more slender, cylindrical fruitbodies. It grows from buried dead branches of broad-leaved trees, especially sycamore.

Old fruitbodies are hard, black, light in weight and shiny, looking like burnt cakes. When cut open they reveal concentric light and dark zones, similar to charcoal. When young they are red-brown, heavy and have a matt surface. They are hemispherical or cushion-shaped; often lobed but stalkless, the fruitbody being attached by a broad, flat area.

SIZE 2–7 cm across.

HABITAT Attached to dead wood of broad-leaved trees; mostly on ash.

SEASON Summer to autumn. Old ones persist for many years.

INEDIBLE A folk remedy to relieve night cramp and it is called Cramp Balls for this reason.

SIMILAR SPECIES *Ustulina deusta* forms grey-black crusts on dead stumps, especially of beech.

Diatrype disciformis

Common – but often overlooked – on beech, where the tiny, hard, dark-brown to black, circular or polygonal, disc-shaped fruitbodies burst through the bark. Hundreds together make a regular pattern and darken the colour of the bark. A lens reveals that the flat upper surface of the disc is roughened.

SIZE 2–3 mm diameter.
HABITAT Gregarious and pushing through the bark of small dead branches of beech. Rare on other broad-leaved trees.
SEASON Throughout the year.
INEDIBLE Mostly buried in bark.
SIMILAR SPECIES *Hypoxylon fragiforme* forms small, hard, brown lumps on the bark of dead beech. *H. multiforme* forms grey, wart-like lumps on birch bark.

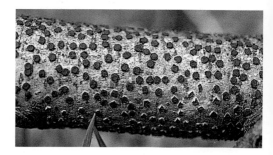